Moving the Earth

ACKNOWLEDGEMENTS

Thank you to all the teachers who evaluated and/or tested these lessons: Hilary Ernst, Anna Flynn, Mary Gerke, Pamela Gerke, Claudia Krase and Alina Rossano.

Thank you to Daniel Johnson, Krista Harris and Bette Lamont for providing information on Laban Movement Analysis and Developmental Movement.

Thank you to Anne Green Gilbert and the faculty of Creative Dance Center, Eric Johnson and Alina Rossano for ideas and inspiration.

Thank you to Mary Gerke for her fine illustrations.

Thank you to Marisa Smith, Eric Kraus, Julia Hill, and the staff at Smith and Kraus, Inc. for their help and support in creating this book.

DEDICATION

This book is dedicated to my mother and father, Gloria and Bernard Rimland, who have made everything in my life possible.

Published by Smith and Kraus, Inc.
PO Box 127, Lyme, NH 03768

Manufactured in the United States of America
Cover and Text Design by Julia Hill

First Edition: June 1997
10 9 8 7 6 5 4 3 2 1

The Library of Congress Cataloging-In-Publication Data
Landalf, Helen.
Moving the earth: teaching earth science through movement
for grades 3–6 / by Helen Landalf. —1st ed.
p. cm. — (Young actors series)
Includes bibliographical references.
ISBN 1-57525-108-6
1. Earth sciences—Study and teaching (Elementary)
2. Movement education. I. Title. II. Series: Young actor series.
QE40.L29 1997
372.3'5—dc21 97-11379
CIP

Moving the Earth

Teaching Earth Science Through Movement for Grades 3–6

by Helen Landalf
illustrated by Mary Gerke

Young Actors Series

Smith and Kraus, Inc.

Contents

Introductory Material

Introduction vi

Moving the Earth vii
- The Arts in Education viii
- Movement as a Learning Tool ix
- Movement and the Body ix
- Movement and the Brain x
- Movement and the Mind xi
- Movement and the Emotions xi
- Movement and Interpersonal Skills xi
- Movement and Earth Science xii

Chart Movement Concepts xii
Chart A Partial Listing of Locomotor and Non-locomotor Movements xiii

What are Movement Concepts? xiv

How to Use this Book xxi
- Using This Book Within Your Existing Earth Science Program xxi
- Preparing Your Students for Movement-Based Science Lessons xxii
- Using the Earth Science Lessons xxiii
- Managing Movement xxviii

The Earth Science Lessons

INTRODUCTORY LESSONS 1
- *Lesson 1a: Methods Used by Scientists* 2
- *Lesson 1b: The Earth is Always Changing* 4

PART I
WHAT IS THE EARTH? 7
- *Lesson 2: Interrelated Spheres* 8

Section A: Earth's Interior 11
- *Lesson 3: Core, Mantle, Crust* 11

Section B: The Lithosphere 13

UNIT 1: MATTER 13
- *Lesson 4: States of Matter* 14
- *Lesson 5: Properties of Matter* 16
- *Lesson 6: Elements, Compounds and Mixtures* . 18

UNIT 2: MINERALS 21
- *Lesson 7: Properties of Minerals* 21

UNIT 3: ROCKS 24
- *Lesson 8: Classes of Rock* 25
- *Lesson 9: The Rock Cycle* 27

Section C: The Atmosphere 30

UNIT 1: STRUCTURE AND FUNCTION OF THE ATMOSPHERE 31
- *Lesson 10: Layers of the Atmosphere* 31
- *Lesson 11: The Oxygen-Carbon Dioxide Cycle* . . . 34

UNIT 2: WEATHER AND CLIMATE 36
- *Lesson 12: Clouds* 36
- *Lesson 13: Air Masses and Fronts* 40
- *Lesson 14: Storms* 43
- *Lesson 15: Climate* 45

UNIT 3: THE SUN'S ENERGY 47
- *Lesson 16: What Happens to Energy from the Sun?* 48

Section D: The Hydrosphere 51

UNIT 1: THE WATER CYCLE 51
- *Lesson 17: The Water Cycle* 52

UNIT 2: FRESHWATER 54
- *Lesson 18: Freshwater Vocabulary* 54
- *Lesson 19: The Life of a River* 56

UNIT 3: THE OCEAN 58
- *Lesson 20: Ocean Topography* 60
- *Lesson 21: Water Pressure* 63
- *Lesson 22: Tides* 65

The Earth Science Lessons *cont.*

PART II THE CHANGING FACE OF THE EARTH . . . 67

Section A: Weathering, Erosion and Deposition . . . 68

UNIT 1: WEATHERING . . . 68
Lesson 23: Physical Weathering . . . 69
Lesson 24: Chemical Weathering . . . 71

UNIT 2: EROSION . . . 72
Lesson 25: Weathering and Erosion . . . 73
Lesson 26: Agents of Erosion . . . 75

UNIT 3: DEPOSITION . . . 76
Lesson 27: Deposited Landforms . . . 78

Section B: Plate Tectonics . . . 80

UNIT 1: EARTH PLATES . . . 81
Lesson 28: Earth Plate Movement . . . 81

UNIT 2: MOUNTAIN-BUILDING . . . 84
Lesson 29: Mountain-Building . . . 84

Section C: Volcanoes . . . 87
Lesson 30: Causes of Volcanic Activity . . . 87
Lesson 31: Volcanic Landforms . . . 89

CONCLUDING LESSONS . . . 93
Lesson 32: Natural Disasters . . . 94
Lesson 33: Earth Science Review . . . 96

Appendices

Creating Your Own Movement-Based Science Lessons . . . 98

Glossary . . . 101

Discography . . . 105

Bibliography . . . 107

Sample Creative Dance Lessons
Lesson 1: Speed . . . 109
Lesson 2: Balance . . . 110

List of Illustrations

fig. 1: Interrelated Spheres Floor Plan . . . 9

fig. 2: Cleavage and Fracture of Minerals . . . 22

fig. 3: The Rock Cycle . . . 28

fig. 4: Rock Cycle Segments (examples) . . . 29

fig. 5: Layers of the Atmosphere . . . 32

fig. 6: Cloud Types . . . 38

fig. 7: Underwater Landforms . . . 59

fig. 8: Deposited Landforms . . . 77

fig. 9: Convergence of Two Continental Plates . . . 82

fig. 10: Volcanic Landforms . . . 90

Introduction

I am not an earth scientist. I am however, foolishly or not, a dance educator who loves to rush in where wiser folk fear to tread.

In the winter of 1995 I was preparing to spend three weeks in the Helena, Montana Public Schools as an Artist-In-Residence through the Arts Plus Program. This program, sponsored by Helena Presents and the Montana Arts Council, brings professional artists into the public schools to educate and inspire the students about the artist's chosen form of expression, whether it be dance, drama, music or visual art. In preparation for spending a week with a class of elementary-grade students, I usually ask the classroom teacher what particular topics his or her students are studying at the time of my dance residency so that I can make an attempt to integrate those topics into my dance lessons.

I was fully confident that the fourth grade teacher at Ray Bjork Elementary School would ask me to integrate mathematics or spelling into my dance lessons, and that I would be able to rely on some tried and true activities for teaching those topics through movement. However, when I received a letter from the principal at Ray Bjork saying that the fourth grade teacher had requested that I integrate dance and earth science, my first response was "What is earth science?" I asked the principal to send me a few chapters from the fourth grade science textbook so I would have some idea of what I was getting myself into.

A week later I received an envelope in the mail with three chapters from the fourth grade science book: one on volcanoes, one on warm and cold fronts and one on earth plates. As I read through the lessons my original trepidation changed to excitement. I could immediately see possibilities for presenting this material powerfully through movement. I made a trip to the public library and immersed myself in learning about such topics as erosion, weathering, plate tectonics and the rock cycle.

Finally the week arrived when I was to begin my residency with the fourth grade class at Ray Bjork Elementary. I was, admittedly, more than a little nervous because I was trying something I had never attempted before. I began with a dance lesson on Shapes—straight, curved, angular and twisted, and integrated the idea of what happens when two earth plates spread apart, collide or slide past each other. As the students worked in pairs to show the movement of earth plates I could see that something exciting was happening—they were engaged in creating and expressing themselves based on something that they had formerly only grasped intellectually. As their teacher watched them work she turned to me and said, "They will never forget what earth plates do."

On Friday, the final day of the week-long residency, the fourth graders performed for the entire school. Using the basic Movement Concepts as a foundation, they danced about earth plates and erosion, volcanoes and storms. Their excitement about what they had learned was evident.

I had another agenda while I was in Montana which was to decide on a new book to propose to my publisher, Smith and Kraus, Inc. I had been toying with several ideas, but nothing had quite yet sparked my interest and passion. After my experience with the fourth graders at Ray Bjork I sat down and wrote a proposal for a book called *Moving the Earth: Teaching Earth Science Through Movement in Grades 3–6.* And so began the journey of creating this book.

I am not an earth scientist, but I am an educator who is willing to take the risk of trying something new, and to do whatever it takes to lead young people into a fuller involvement in learning. Perhaps using movement as a means of presenting academic concepts is as foreign to you as earth science, at the outset, was to me. My hope is that this book will serve as a guide and inspiration for you, as a teacher, to go courageously into uncharted territory; to go beyond your fears of the unknown to uncover the treasure of potential that lies waiting within each one of your students. For journeying into the unknown is what science—and education—are all about.

Moving the Earth

Changes on the planet Earth are incomprehensibly slow. It has taken approximately 4,500 million years for the earth to transform from a cloud of dust and gas into the spectacular, life-sustaining home that we know today. The present day human body has been a full twenty-five million years in the making.

Changes in the field of education also seem to move at a glacial speed. The children of the '90s are still being educated under a paradigm that was created near the turn of the century, when public education was seen as a way to supply the nation's industries with efficient, compliant workers. Granted, differences have arisen in schools and teaching methods since that time. There is much more emphasis now on the development of problem-solving skills, critical thinking and values education than there was in the past. However, in spite of these changes, many things remain the same. If you peek into a typical elementary classroom today you will most likely see rows of children sitting quietly at desks listening or reading. These largely passive methods of receiving information are our children's heritage from the past.

Fortunately, there is now a small but growing community of educators who believe in the value of using the arts as educational tools. These educators have experienced firsthand the enthusiasm and motivation that arts integration brings to the classroom. They know that the arts provide students not only with access to new knowledge, but with an increased sense of self-esteem, community and a lifelong love of learning.

THE ARTS IN EDUCATION

Children learn best when they are fully invested in learning; when they perceive a given educational task as being what they choose to do. What most children choose to do consistently in their lives is to create. While our culture encourages very young children to express themselves creatively through painting, music and dramatic play, we expect children over the age of six to "get serious" and leave creativity behind or relegate it to a compartmentalized activity such as a classroom art project or after-school music lessons. In doing so we overlook a powerful tool for inspiring students to search for and assimilate knowledge.

When the arts are used as an educational tool students are given the opportunity to not merely take in information, but synthesize it into a new form. When children are asked to interact creatively with a subject they are studying rather than to simply hear a lecture, see a video or read a book, they begin to make the information their own. A child who uses curricular content as a springboard for creative self-expression begins to build a bridge between his or her own thoughts and the material being presented.

Some teachers are reluctant to invite the arts into their classrooms because they see the arts as being "frills"; superfluous distractions to the real business of learning. This is far from the truth. Integrating the arts into the curriculum fosters the coveted skills of analysis, critical thinking and problem-solving. In order to create an artistic form of expression based on a curricular topic, the student must be able to analyze that topic and break it into its component parts. The student must use problem-solving skills to relate the topic to the art form being used and must think critically in order to evaluate and refine his or her artistic creation. All of these skills are employed willingly and naturally by the student striving to create an outward expression of an internal idea.

In addition to the valuable skills mentioned above, integrating the arts into the curriculum also fosters creativity and imagination. As an added bonus, students develop a sense of community with their peers when they work together to express themselves artistically. Their self-esteem grows as they see that their unique contributions are respected and valued by others.

All of these benefits might be reason enough for the arts to be used as teaching tools in every classroom. But current brain research gives us even more compelling evidence that the inclusion of the arts is not only desirable but critical to the development of powerful, effective minds.

Scientists have long been aware that the two hemispheres of the brain serve vastly different functions. While the left brain processes language and numbers, applies logic and analyzes data—the functions most commonly used in traditional education—the right brain houses imagination and emotion, searches for patterns and synthesizes components into a meaningful whole—all demands made on the brain by the artistic process. Though for a time it was believed that these two hemispheres functioned independently, it is now clear that the functioning of both hemispheres together is what gives the human mind its flexibility and unique power. Therefore, the most effective education a child can have is one that addresses both hemispheres of the brain and demands that they work together. This is exactly what happens when music, visual art, theater and dance are integrated into the basic curriculum.

An additional important reason for the inclusion of arts in the curriculum is that the arts are motivating to students. Activities involving the arts are fun! Students willingly engage in activities that they enjoy, and remember those activities and the curricular topics they are based upon. Inclusion of the arts makes learning a joyful and exciting process.

MOVEMENT AS A LEARNING TOOL

Of all the art forms—music, visual arts, theater and dance—dance is the art form least frequently employed in the classroom. There are several reasons for this. One reason is that dance requires open space, which is at a premium in most school buildings. Another, probably more prevalent reason is that most teachers feel that they have inadequate training to provide dance experiences for their students. Dance is seen as an elitist art form which only a few highly trained and talented individuals are fit to engage in.

It is important at this point to make a distinction between dance as an art form and movement as a learning tool. Though the terms "dance" and "movement" may seem to be interchangeable, they are not. For the purposes of this book "dance" is an art form in which movements of the body are used to express thoughts, ideas and feelings. In dance any curricular content or topic (i.e.: Earth Science) is secondary and in service of aesthetic self-expression. "Movement," on the other hand, refers to movements of the body which are being used as a tool to enhance understanding of a curricular topic. In this case the form of expression is secondary to or in service of the curricular content. Most of the activities in this book fall into the latter (movement) category, though a few of the choreographic problems will elicit solutions that approach the art form of dance. The term "movement study" is used when students are asked to create a sequence of movements which are primarily a product of the content of the lesson, and secondarily of artistic expression.

As teachers who use it regularly will attest, movement is an incredibly effective learning tool. Movement experiences actively engage students physically, mentally, emotionally and socially. Movement truly fosters the development of the whole child.

MOVEMENT AND THE BODY

It should be quite obvious that movement experiences can benefit the physical development of a child. Movement activities help students develop body awareness, strength and flexibility as well as balance and coordination. The student who has the opportunity for movement on a regular basis will improve his or her gross motor skills, develop strong, flexible muscles and increase stamina. In addition, movement provides an opportunity for the release of pent-up energy and sends blood flowing throughout the system, increasing oxygen to the brain. The physical release provided by moving can help a student concentrate more easily on academic subjects.

Engaging in movement activities that are challenging, creative and satisfying encourages children to value physical activity and seek to make it a part of their lives. In the current age of television and computers it is vitally important that young people enjoy and appreciate using their bodies. Being physically active leads to a healthier lifestyle and a fuller participation in living.

MOVEMENT AND THE BRAIN

Although most people would readily agree that movement helps build muscles and increase stamina, many would be surprised to learn that it also helps develop that all-important part of our body, the brain. This becomes most obvious when we look at how an infant grows and develops: every phase in an infant's development of sensory perception, language comprehension and acquisition and even organization of thought itself corresponds to the mastery of a physical movement. As a child progresses from an infant squirming on its back to a toddler taking its first steps he or she is not only developing physically, but accessing new areas of the brain.

By the time they reach the third grade most children have completed the progression of physical development that began in infancy. They are adept at many forms of physical movement, they understand and use language with ease and have developed higher order thinking skills. Yet many of these children, who have developed normally in most ways, suffer from hyperactivity, learning disorders and a plethora of other problems which stand in the way of their optimal functioning as human beings. While there are certainly many possible causes for these disorders, research has shown that they often stem from the fact that the child, for some reason, did not experience each stage of the natural movement progression that is linked to brain development. So, in fact, we can actually disable a child by not allowing him or her to move.

There is a great deal of evidence that such disorders can be treated by encouraging the child to re-experience the developmental phase that he or she missed. By repeating the movements natural to that stage of development the brain has a renewed opportunity to form the neurological pathways needed for optimal mental and physical performance. A few of the movements that are particularly beneficial for children to perform are crawling (moving on the belly), creeping (walking on hands and knees), homolateral movement (moving one side of the body at a time, as in moving the right arm and right leg simultaneously), cross-lateral movement (two-sided movement, as in stepping forward with the right leg while reaching forward with the left arm) and movements that stimulate the vestibular system such as spinning, turning and swinging. While encouraging such movements is not the primary purpose of the activities in this book, your students will probably engage in many of them in the natural course of participating in the lessons.

MOVEMENT AND THE MIND

Using movement as a learning tool in the classroom engages children in problem-solving. If you look through the Earth Science lessons in this book you will notice that they are full of questions to be answered through movement: "How might you move if you were the dense, slowly flowing material inside the earth? How will you show that you are a snowflake drifting slowly to the ground? How will you show that you and your partner are two earth plates under such great pressure that they fold and form a mountain range?"

In answering questions such as these students need to take information from two separate bodies of knowledge (movement and Earth Science) and integrate them to form a solution. This is the same process that we, as adults, use in our lives when we seek to use what we already know to extrapolate to a solution that is unknown. For example, if I seek to discover how to get my car to start in cold weather I integrate what I know about automobiles and what I know about weather to find a solution.

As you share these Earth Science lessons with your students you may notice several students who seem to "take" to movement more than others. (They may also be the students who have difficulty focusing when asked to sit still and listen.) These students could be kinesthetic learners: those who receive information primarily through movement and touch. It is very important to provide movement experiences regularly in your classroom in order to reach these learners. You will also find that many of your students will retain information more easily if you teach it through movement. This is because movement involves children in learning actively rather than just listening passively.

MOVEMENT AND THE EMOTIONS

In contrast to athletics, which tends to treat movement as purely functional, the experiences in this book will lead a child toward using movement as a form of self-expression, thus involving his or her emotions. The lessons encourage students to explore and create their own movements within a structure rather than asking them to simply imitate the teacher, thus removing anxiety about doing something the "right" way. Because many varying responses can be correct, students are encouraged to grow in their sense of self-esteem as well as to value the uniqueness and diversity of others.

Your students' movement responses to the challenges these lessons pose will be highly personal. Their choices will reflect their ongoing personal movement preferences, as well as how they are feeling at any particular moment. By giving them the opportunity to express the uniqueness of their spirits in movement, you will be opening a powerful new avenue for self-expression in their lives.

MOVEMENT AND INTERPERSONAL SKILLS

In addition to increasing self-awareness, movement activities can also develop positive interactions between students. Sharing space with others, observing and valuing a diversity of movement choices and working together to solve problems all serve to increase the respect and caring of students for their classmates. As they work in small and large groups to create movement studies, children also develop the skills of leadership, initiative, negotiation and collaboration.

MOVEMENT AND EARTH SCIENCE

The earth is always changing: rocks are changing into new types of rocks, material from inside the earth rises to the surface, water evaporates into the atmosphere, the oceans wear away the land. Earth Science is all about the process of change, and movement is change—from one shape to another, from one place to another, from one relationship to another. This makes movement the perfect vehicle for teaching Earth Science. Teaching Earth Science through movement allows children to actually embody the processes that continually transform our planet. What children experience with their own bodies they are more likely to remember, to value and to care for.

In today's world we are playing for high stakes—for the education of our children, who will need an incomprehensibly sophisticated set of skills to enable them to cope with an unknown future, for the continued honor of the amazing human body whose use is declining in the age of information, and for the survival of the beleaguered planet itself. If we can keep these stakes in view and teach our children with all the passion and urgency that they demand, we will truly move the earth.

MOVEMENT CONCEPTS

BODY

Body Parts:	Head, Arms, Elbows, Hands, Back, Stomach, Legs, Feet, etc.
Body Shape:	Straight, Curved, Angular, Twisted, Wide, Narrow
Balance:	On Balance, Off Balance

SPACE

Place:	Self Space, General Space
Level:	High, Middle, Low
Direction:	Forward, Backward, Right, Left, Up, Down
Pathway:	Straight, Curved, Zig-zag
Size:	Big, Medium, Little
Relationship:	Over, Under, Around, Through, Together, Apart, etc.

QUALITY

Speed:	Slow, Medium, Fast
Rhythm:	Pulse, Breath, Pattern
Weight:	Strong, Light
Energy:	Smooth, Sharp
Flow:	Free, Bound
Focus:	Single focus, Multi-focus

A PARTIAL LISTING OF LOCOMOTOR AND NON-LOCOMOTOR MOVEMENTS

Locomotor (traveling)

crawl
gallop
hop
jump
leap
roll
run
scoot
skip
slide
slither
walk

Non-Locomotor (stationary)

bend squirm
carve stretch
dab swing
flick turn
float twist
glide wriggle
poke wring
press
punch
shake
slash
spin

Using this chart

The words on this chart may be called out as suggestions during any portion of a lesson in which students are moving freely. For example: if students are exploring moving as a liquid in Lesson 4: States of Matter, in addition to cueing them with the Movement Concepts on the preceding page ("Could your liquid flow in different Directions? Will your liquid change its Level?") you can invite them to incorporate various locomotor and non-locomotor movements into their exploration. ("How might you leap if you were a liquid? What would a liquidy turn look like?") Being reminded of these words as they explore will help students vary the kind of movements they choose to do instead of always walking or running.

It is highly recommended that you make a large copy of both this chart and the Movement Concepts chart to display whenever you are doing a movement / science activity so that you can refer to them easily while teaching. Your students will also find it helpful to refer to the charts when creating and evaluating choreography.

What are Movement Concepts?

The basic movement concepts discussed in this book were originally defined and recorded by Rudolph von Laban in the 1930s in his attempt to describe and analyze movement and to establish a notation system for movement similar to the one used to notate music. These concepts underlie all movements, whether they be dance steps, athletic feats, pedestrian movements or even the movements of animals or machines.

Over the years many variations of Laban's vocabulary have evolved and many movement educators, myself included, no longer adhere strictly to his original terminology. In this book I use vocabulary similar to that developed by Anne Green Gilbert, an internationally recognized dance educator and founder of the Creative Dance Center in Seattle, Washington. Though my organization of the concepts is slightly different from Gilbert's, it is similar enough to make this book compatible with her highly recommended materials. (See Bibliography.) For the purposes of this book I will divide the concepts into the following three areas:

Body—including the Parts of the body that can move and the Shapes that the body can take.

Space—where the body moves in space, including the Level, Direction, Pathway and Size of a movement.

Quality—whether the movement is slow or fast, strong or light, smooth or sharp, etc.

The following section contains a short description of each Movement Concept, followed by a simple idea for exploring the concept with students in the upper elementary grades. You may want to read the entire section once to acquaint yourself with all of the concepts. It is also suggested that you refresh your memory by reviewing the related concept(s) before teaching one of the movement-based Earth Science lessons in this book. This will facilitate your ability to present the lesson clearly to your students. For a complete listing of the concepts see the Movement Concepts chart at the beginning of this chapter.

BODY

All of the concepts in the area of Body define how the body itself moves, exclusive of the body's relationship to space, time or other people. Since the body will be the instrument for learning and self-expression in the following Earth Science lessons, this area of movement will always be at play, even if not referred to directly. For pre-adolescents, who are dealing with a changing sense of their physical selves, the Body is an essential concept to explore.

Body Parts:

Head, Neck, Shoulders, Spine, Arms, Elbows, Hands, Stomach, Hips, Leg, Feet, etc.

The body can be divided into many different parts which can be moved in isolation (i.e.: standing still while only moving your head), in combination (i.e.: moving elbows and knees simultaneously) or moving all parts together as one unit. Body parts can lead us through space, move us along the floor and help us create shapes.

Idea for Exploring: Have students stand in one place. Call out the name of a body part (i.e.: "elbows"). When music plays, students will move only that part. When the music stops, they stop their movement and listen for the next body part to be called.

Shapes:

Straight, Curved, Angular, Twisted, Wide, Narrow, Symmetrical, Asymmetrical

Our bodies can make shapes. If we stretch all of our body parts, a straight shape is created. When we bend our joints we are making an angular shape. Softening or rotating our body parts creates shapes that are curved or twisted. Shapes can also be wide, narrow, symmetrical (the same on both sides) or asymmetrical (different on each side).

Shapes can remain stationary, like a still photograph in one spot, or they can move through space. It is also possible for us to change shapes while we are moving. We can make shapes alone or with other dancers.

Idea for Exploring: Divide students into pairs with one student being a sculptor and the other student the clay. The sculptor molds the clay into a shape, then copies that shape. Reverse roles. You may ask sculptors to make one of the specific types of shapes listed above, or encourage them to create their own.

Balance:

On, Off

When our body is on balance, as when we're standing with two feet planted firmly on the floor, we feel stable and connected to the ground. When our body is off balance, as when we lean or tip, we feel as if we might fall. The challenge is to go off balance, but still be in control.

We can make many kinds of balancing shapes: balancing on one foot, on a hand and a foot, on a bottom, etc. We can also go off balance as we move by tipping, swirling or spinning on one leg.

Idea for Exploring: Encourage students to experiment with the many types of balancing shapes they can create. Call out specific body parts for them to place on the floor (i.e.: "Balance on one foot...two hands and one foot...your stomach... your back"). Or, simply call out a number or equation and let them place that number—or the equation's solution—of body parts on the floor. In this case they would independently choose which body parts to use. For example: if you call out the equation "twelve divided by four", some students will show the solution "three" by balancing on two feet and one hand, others on two hands and one foot, others on two elbows and one knee, etc.

SPACE

The concept area of Space defines the expanse we are moving through and how we get from one place to another. The same principles of Space apply whether we are moving in a large gymnasium or in a small corner of a classroom. The more students understand about their relationship to space, the more orderly and less confusing the physical world will seem to confusing the physical world will seem to them.

Place:

Self Space, General Space

The concept of Place tells us whether we're moving on one spot (Self Space) or traveling through space (General Space). Movement done in place is called non-locomotor movement while traveling steps are known as locomotor movements. (See listing of Locomotor and Non-locomotor Movements preceding this chapter.) Whether we travel or stay in one place, we have a personal space or kinesphere which serves as a boundary between our own space and the space of others. Our kinesphere is like a giant bubble that surrounds our body. It can expand or shrink, depending on how much space is available to move in and how close to others we feel comfortable being in any given situation.

Young people who are exposed to the concept of Place will find it easier to move in the vicinity of others without bumping or crashing. By giving them the option to move in one spot and encouraging them to find empty spaces as they visualize their own kinesphere and the kinespheres of others, they become more aware of their placement in the room and more responsible in their relationships to other movers.

Idea for Exploring: Have students stand in self space, facing a partner. The leader will move slowly in self space while the partner mirrors (copies) their movement. Both partners will dance away from each other in general space, then return to mirroring with the second partner as leader. This works best with a piece of music which has alternating phrases (see Discography).

Size:

Big, Medium, Little

As we move in self or general space, we can vary the amount of area our movement takes up. Big movements reach far into space with the body parts stretching wide, while little movements stay very close to the center of the body. We change the size of a shape or movement by growing or shrinking. It is important to note that "big" is not synonymous with "tall"—it is possible to make a big shape by lying on the floor with body parts stretched far apart. We can, in the same way, remain standing and be "little" by holding our body parts close together.

Students who naturally do very big movements, often unintentionally knocking things over or hurting others, can learn to be more careful by being given an opportunity to practice small movements. Young people who are shy or timid may find it easier to be more confident and assertive if they have a chance to practice large movements. It is also helpful to practice growing and shrinking; gradating between big and small.

Idea for Exploring: Ask students to dance with very large movements, taking up as much space as possible. Then ask them to imagine that the room is shrinking, and that they have to make their movements smaller and smaller so as not to bump into the walls.

Directions:

Forward, Backward, Right, Left, Up, Down

We can move through general space in any of the six directions listed above. Direction is determined by the surface of the body that is leading us through space: the front of the body leads us forward, the back of our body leads us backward, the sides of our body lead us right and left, the top of our body leads us up and the bottom of our body leads us down.

It is important to differentiate "direction" from "facing," which is determined by a place in the room. For example, you might be facing a window, moving forward toward it, but you could also turn your back to the window and move backward to it. You could also turn, face another side of the room and move forward toward the new facing.

Idea for Exploring: Pairs of students stand with one student in front of the other. The leading student moves through the room in varying directions, followed by their partner. The leader always keeps his or her back to their partner, which requires caution and awareness when moving backward. At your signal or when the music changes the other student becomes the leader.

Levels:

Low, Middle, High

Level determines whether we are close to the ground or far away. Low level movement is very close to the floor. Slithering, creeping (on hands and knees) and rolling are common low level movements. In high level movement the body is at its full height or in the air. Walking on tiptoe, skipping and leaping are examples of high level movement. Middle level movement is movement in between low and high. Some examples of middle level movement are walking crouched over, walking on one's knees with the body upright or "crab-walking" (hands and feet on the floor, stomach toward the ceiling).

We can also change levels as we move. Rising is the action of changing from low level to high and sinking is the action of changing from high level to low.

Idea for Exploring: Using a prop for each student such as a scarf or crepe paper streamer, call out a level for the students' bodies and a level for their prop, for example: "Body high, scarf low." Or "Body middle, scarf high." Allow the students a minute or two to find varying ways to move with each body / prop combination before going on to the next one.

Pathways:

Straight, Curved, Zig-zag

Pathways are the designs our body parts create as they move through space and the designs our feet make as we move across the floor. You might think of your pathway as the "jet stream" you leave behind as you move. When you move in straight pathways you are moving only in straight lines and turning corners sharply. Curved pathways can take the form of circles, spirals or waves. Zig-zag pathways are straight pathways that change direction sharply, as in the contours of lightning or mountain ranges. Pathways can be created on the floor with the feet (or other body parts if moving at a low or middle level) or in the air by moving arms, heads, elbows, etc.

Idea for Exploring: Ask each student to create a simple line drawing incorporat-

ing each of the three pathways, then use the drawing as a map to design movements that travel through the room. This can be done individually or in trios, with each student contributing a different pathway to the drawing.

Relationships:

Near, Far, Over, Under, Around, Through, Above, Below, On, Off, etc.

As we move, we are creating relationships between our body parts. We might be moving with all of our body parts near each other, with our arms overhead, or with our hands on our hips. In addition, we may choose to create relationships with objects (a chair, a scarf, a balloon) or with other people. Sometimes all three types of relationships may be happening at once!

Relationships can happen in stillness and in movement. For example, you might make a still shape over a scarf or skip around a partner. When having relationships with other movers we can relate to one person (a partner) or a group of people. It is possible for partners or groups to move over, under, around and through each other. Moving in relationship to others requires awareness and cooperation, essential elements in building social skills.

Idea for Exploring: Have half of the students make frozen shapes in empty spots in the room. When the music begins the remaining students will move over, under, around and through the shapes. When the music stops the dancers will choose one shape to create a relationship with. For example, if the original shape is wide and open, the dancer might make a smaller shape to fit inside. When the music begins again the shapes become the dancers and the dancers make new shapes.

QUALITY

The concept area of Quality defines how a movement is performed: slowly or quickly, strongly or lightly, smoothly or sharply, etc. Movement researcher Rudolph von Laban called this area of movement "Effort" because of the varying degrees of energy required to complete specific types of movements. The quality of a movement is affected by the inner image our mind holds while moving (i.e.: "lightly as a feather"). Quality can also be affected by an attitude or feeling (i.e.: feeling luxurious when moving slowly, feeling urgent when moving quickly.)

Speed:

Slow, Medium, Fast

The speed or tempo at which your body moves determines how much time it takes you to complete a movement. Some movements tend to be done slowly, such as floating, melting and stretching. Other movements are usually done at a fast speed: running, shaking, spinning. A large number of movements can be done at any speed. For example: walking, turning and twisting could each be done very slowly, extremely quickly or at any speed in between. Each of these movements could also accelerate (get faster and faster) or decelerate (become progressively slower.)

Many young people tend to move quite quickly and find it a challenge to slow down. For this reason, moving at a variety of speeds is important to practice often.

Idea for Exploring: After asking students to explore moving their entire bodies extremely slowly then extremely quickly, ask them to try moving their upper bodies (heads, torso and arms) slowly while moving the lower body (legs and pelvis) quickly. The reverse is even trickier!

Rhythm:

Pulse, Breath, Pattern

Rhythm is the pattern our movements make in time. The rhythm of our movement can be an even pulse, like a heartbeat, or free flowing and varied like our breath. When we divide time into beats of different lengths we create a rhythmic pattern.

Students in the upper elementary grades enjoy and benefit from both analyzing and learning about rhythm, and responding freely to music with different rhythms.

Idea for Exploring: Play a simple, repeated rhythmic pattern on a drum, for example: slow, slow, quick, quick, quick, quick (half-note, half-note, quarter, quarter, quarter, quarter). Allow students to spontaneously create movement patterns that relate to the rhythm. One student's movement might be: twist, twist, jump, jump, jump, jump. Another student's response might be: Curl, stretch, turn, turn, slash, slash. After most students seem to have created a satisfying pattern, try again with a new rhythm.

Weight:

Strong, Light

The quality of Weight defines how we are using our muscles as we move—either with strength and power or lightly and delicately. There are two ways of moving with strong weight. When we use strong weight actively we contract our muscles and press, pull, punch or slash. When we use strong weight passively our muscles are limp and our bodies are heavy, giving in to the pull of gravity. Light movement requires withholding part of one's weight to produce a delicate, lifted feeling. Examples of light movement are floating, flicking, dabbing and scampering. However, many movements can be done either strongly or lightly.

Idea for Exploring: Have pairs of students practice sharing their weight. Standing one to two feet apart and facing each other, students press their palms together and lean into each other. The object is for them to share weight equally without one partner overpowering the other. After mastering this shape the partners can explore sharing weight between other body parts: shoulders, backs, feet, etc.

Energy:

Smooth, Sharp

When our Energy is smooth, our movement is ongoing, without stops. Another name for this is "sustained" movement. In contrast, sharp movement is full of quick stops. It can also be called "percussive" or "sudden" movement.

Imagery is often helpful in evoking smooth or sharp movement. Some images for smooth movement might be: painting a wall, clouds floating, birds gliding through the air. Some images for sharp movement might be: punching an enemy, popping a balloon, swatting a fly.

Idea for Exploring: Using balloons, have the students alternate between smooth and sharp movement. They could float, swirl, turn and roll with their balloons smoothly, then bat, tap and kick them sharply. After repeating this exploration several times, challenge them to try it without the balloons! Music with alternating legato and staccato sections works well for this exploration.

Flow:

Free, Bound

When we move with free flow we move with abandon, allowing the movement to flow through our bodies without trying to control or stop it. This might have the sensation of wind or water moving through our bodies and is very smooth and ongoing. Bound flow, by contrast, is very controlled. This could take the form of jerky, robot-like movement or movement with extreme caution or control, as in walking a tightrope. Flow, like all movement qualities, exists on a continuum—absolutely free, moderately free, slightly free to slightly bound, moderately bound, extremely bound.

Some of your students (or yourself!) may tend to move through life in a free-flowing way—"going with the flow" with very little pre-planning, and perhaps being physically reckless. These students can benefit greatly by practicing bound flow movement.

On the other hand, you may also have students who seem very cautious and controlled, afraid to take any risks. These students can open up a great deal through experiencing free-flowing movement. Experiencing the continuum—gradating from one extreme to the other—is helpful for both types of people.

Idea for Exploring: Have students move freely, imagining that a wind is blowing them around the room or that they are a flowing river. Contrast this with moving like robots or machines, keeping their bodies very controlled.

Focus:

Single Focus, Multi-Focus

Focus defines how we direct our attention as we move. When we use single focus, all of our attention is directed toward one thing at a time. We may simply look at one object, place or person or may reach toward it or move toward it. We can change our point of focus very rapidly but as long as we focus on one thing at a time we are using single focus.

When we allow our attention to widen we are using multi-focus. This is when we direct our attention toward may things at once. We might imagine that we are scanning a horizon. Our eyes may look at many places in the room and our body might be turning or weaving in space.

Idea for Exploring: Students mirror a partner in self space (see Idea for Exploring the concept Place), focusing strongly on that partner. Call out a specific point of focus as they dance away from each other through general space (i.e.: "focus on your hand," "focus on the window," "focus on another person," "focus all around the room"). When they return to each other the second partner will be the leader for mirroring.

A FINAL NOTE: Though each concept has been described here separately, the Movement Concepts never function in isolation. Even in the simple act of walking across the room you will be using several different concepts at once: you may be walking in a forward Direction at a high Level and a fast Speed through general Space! The combining of Movement Concepts is what makes the possibilities of movement infinitely creative and exciting.

How to Use this Book

If you are like many classroom teachers, the lessons in this book may be very different from the types of activities you usually engage in with your students. Or, if you are lucky enough to be working in a school or district where teachers are supported in integrating the arts into the curriculum, this type of material may be more familiar to you. In either case this chapter will help guide you in determining how movement-based activities can fit into your existing Earth Science curriculum, how to prepare your students to engage in movement activities successfully, and how to most effectively present the lessons in this book.

USING THIS BOOK WITHIN YOUR EXISTING EARTH SCIENCE PROGRAM

It should be emphasized at the outset that the material in this book is intended to supplement and expand upon your existing Earth Science curriculum, not to replace it. Our efforts to teach the whole child need to include the verbal-linguistic intelligence (reading, listening, speaking and writing) as well as the kinesthetic intelligence, which is accessed through movement and touch. In order to provide as broad a range of experiences to your students as possible, you will in addition want to include scientific experimentation, specimen study, map-making and field trips as part of your Earth Science program.

The frequency with which you integrate these movement-based lessons into your program will depend upon your prior experience and comfort level with leading movement activities, the experience level of your students, the space in your school building which is available for movement, and the extent to which the content of the lessons matches the content you wish to teach. If you are a teacher who is new to using movement as a teaching tool, you will probably want to start slowly, perhaps using a lesson from this book once every one to two weeks. In this way you will give yourself time to learn and develop your skill and comfort level without feeling overwhelmed.

In choosing lessons from this book to share with your class, make your decisions based on both the content of the lessons and the experience level of your students. It is advisable to begin with lessons that are simple, guided improvisations rather then more complicated group choreographic activities. You may also choose to simplify a more complex lesson by doing only the introductory improvisation, or doing the choreographic activity as a whole class rather than in groups. Your students, too, need to build skills slowly so they can feel safe and comfortable rather than self-conscious and threatened.

PREPARING YOUR STUDENTS FOR MOVEMENT-BASED SCIENCE LESSONS

Just as we would never expect a student to write a short story on the computer without teaching him or her basic computer skills, or to compose a piece of music without knowing about melody, harmony and rhythm, it is unreasonable to expect students to express themselves to their full creative potential in movement without at least a rudimentary knowledge of the Movement Concepts. For this reason it is highly recommended that you take time with your students during the year to experience and explore the Movement Concepts described in the previous chapter. Doing so will greatly improve their enjoyment of and ability to learn from the Earth Science lessons in this book.

The theory and methodology of teaching Creative Dance is certainly too large a subject to be covered in this chapter and several excellent books have been written on the subject, most notably Anne Green Gilbert's *Creative Dance for All Ages* (see Bibliography). I will simply get you started with a format for planning Creative Dance lessons. Two sample lesson plans can be found in the Appendices. Many more lesson plans can be found in Gilbert's book.

A thirty- to sixty-minute Creative Dance lesson for third to sixth graders should include the following components:

Warm-up

An opportunity for students to warm up their muscles through light aerobic movements such as stretching, curling, bending, twisting, swinging and shaking.

Concept Introduction

Introduce students to one of the Movement Concepts described in the previous chapter. Have them say the concept words while briefly experiencing the movements or shapes those word describe. For example, when being introduced to the concept Size the students would say the words "big," "medium," and "little" while making shapes of those sizes with their bodies.

Concept Exploration

In this section of the lesson, students have an opportunity to initially explore the concept and discover how it affects their movement. This can be done individually, in partners or groups, with or without the use of props (scarves, crepe paper streamers, balloons, etc.). There is a suggested concept exploration activity for each Movement Concept under the heading *Idea for Exploring* in the section, "What Are Movement Concepts."

Skill Development

In a well-rounded Creative Dance class, it is important to include not only opportunities for creative exploration, but also activities for the development of physical skills. The skill development section of the lesson could include one or more of the following:

RHYTHM SKILLS:

Developing a sense of rhythm through playing musical instruments to a beat, moving to rhythmic chants or performing movement to counts.

LOCOMOTOR AND NON-LOCOMOTOR SKILLS:
Practicing skills such as skipping, turning, sliding floating, slashing and so on.

LEAPING:
Practicing the skill of leaping is fun and exciting and encourages development of both sides of the body through taking off from one foot and landing on the other. You may want to begin by asking students to leap over stacked objects such as milk cartons or boxes, then take the objects away when they are no longer needed as visual cues.

MOVEMENT COMBINATIONS:
Practicing a sequence of movements or a "dance." This requires students to remember a sequence and to learn to link movements together. A movement combination could be a folk or square dance, a popular dance or a dance you create by making a sentence of locomotor and non-locomotor words. An example of such a dance might be: "skip…melt…roll…rise…turn…leap." These movements could be performed to specific counts or with the students' own timing.

It is important to teach skills by referring to the concept introduced at the beginning of the lesson. For example, if you are teaching the concept Level (High, Middle, Low) you might have the students practice rolling low and leaping high, then do a simple dance that changes levels. Activities such as these will develop skills that reinforce the Movement Concept.

Improvisation or Choreography

Conclude your lesson by allowing students to use the concept they have learned to express themselves creatively through improvising—performing movement spontaneously, or choreographing—pre-planning movement. In a lesson on the concept Pathways (Straight, Curved, Zig-zag) students might improvise in response to famous works of art, spontaneously dancing the Pathways they see. Or, for choreography, you might give small groups art reproductions and ask them to plan and perform movements based on the lines in the paintings.

Students in Grades 3–6 will enjoy and benefit from having a complete Creative Dance class, as described above, once or twice a week with the focus on a different Movement Concept each week. If you feel that this is an impossibility for you to provide, it will be extremely helpful, at the very least, to do the activity described under the heading *Idea for Exploration* in the section entitled, "What Are Movement Concepts?" for each concept, introducing one or two concepts a week.

USING THE EARTH SCIENCE LESSONS

Once you have familiarized yourself with the introductory material in the introductory material on pages i–xxx and have begun to introduce your students to the Movement Concepts, you are ready to start using the Earth Science lessons. The lessons are divided into two main parts. Part I: What is the Earth? deals with the earth's structure, with the states and properties of matter, and with the characteristics of the Lithosphere, the

Atmosphere and the Hydrosphere. Part II: The Changing Face of the Earth includes topics that describe agents of change such as erosion, mountain-building and volcanoes.

Each lesson contains important information under the following headings:

Topic

The specific topic of each lesson can be found in its title at the top of the lesson's first page. That topic is further broken down or described under the heading "Topic."

Once you have chosen a lesson you wish to present, read it carefully several times. Ask yourself what learning experiences on that particular topic you might want to provide to make the lesson as rich and successful as possible. Would it be helpful for the students to read a chapter in their textbook on the topic before doing the movement activity? To see a video? To view a map or photograph or handle a concrete object such as a rock specimen? Providing your students with applicable background material helps "fuel" them for self-expression.

Type of Movement Activity

This heading tells you how the material in the lesson will be presented and how the students will be grouped. There are three types of movement activities included in this book:

Group Shapes: Group activities which are shape oriented, with very little movement through space.

Improvisational Exploration: Teacher-guided activities which involve spontaneous movement through space.

Choreography: Activities in which the teacher presents a structure, then acts as an advisor as the students work in groups to plan and execute their own movement sequences or "dances" within that structure. The choreographic activity concludes with an opportunity for each group to perform their work and receive positive comments from their audience.

Each type of movement activity can be presented for one of the following groupings:

Individual: Individual students explore an idea without necessarily relating to others, though there are others moving in the space with them.

Partner: Two students work together to create shapes, explore an idea or create choreography.

Small Group: Groups of three to six students work together.

Large group: Six or more students work together.

In general, the simplest lessons are those involving individual improvisational exploration because there is a minimal need for students to cooperate, collaborate or adapt to each other. The most complex lessons are those involving large group choreography because they require large groups of students to collaborate creatively in planning a movement study.

Related Concepts

This heading tells you which of the Movement Concepts described on page xii are most involved in the execution of the movement in each lesson. These concepts may or may not be explicitly referred to during the lesson. This heading is provided to give you an opportunity to prepare your students for the lesson's creative demands by introducing them to one or more of the related Movement Concepts.

Materials / Preparation

This heading lets you know if any specific materials or preparation are needed or suggested in order to teach the lesson.

Musical Suggestions

Most of the lessons in this book can be done without music. However, music is very motivating for movement and can help students feel more involved and less self-conscious.

Although a few of the lessons suggest specific musical selections, most lessons name one of four possible categories under the "Musical Suggestions" heading:

Constant, dense
Flowing
Energetic, driving
Light, airy

In the Discography at the end of this book you will find suggested selections for each category. Feel free to use any of those selections, or to use a personal favorite of your own. Be aware that, in general, New Age, classical, ethnic or folk music are more conducive to creative movement than popular music, which tends to elicit stereotyped "hip" movement from students at this age. You will also find instrumental music to be more effective than music with lyrics.

Space Requirements

It is a sad truth that adequate space for movement activities in the typical elementary school building is minimal. It is frustrating to note that, while most schools and districts are willing to spend thousands of dollars on computer equipment, providing space for children to use their most natural learning resource—their own body—is not something most budget planners and administrators would even consider. Therefore it unfortunately becomes the responsibility of the classroom teacher to adjust, adapt, and advocate for change in this vital area.

The information under this heading tells you whether the lesson requires a large, open space such as an empty classroom, gym, stage or outdoor area, or can be done in an open area (the front and /or aisles) of the regular classroom. Though I have tried to adapt as many lessons as possible to the space of the regular classroom, some activities simply lose their impact if the students do not have ample room to move. After all, learning through movement requires...moving!

What can you do to find or create the space you need? Here are a few possibilities:

Be aware of all the open spaces in your school and when they are available, if even for half an hour. Try the music room, gym, lunchroom, stage, computer lab, library, etc.

Do a movement activity outdoors on a mild day.

Create a routine for clearing as much space as possible in your classroom. Challenge students to rearrange the furniture in record amounts of time (and put it back when the lesson is over.)

If all of these suggestions fail and you find yourself stuck in a regular classroom with the desks in rows, try the following:

1. Do the movement activity moving up and down the aisles.

2. Whenever possible, change general space (traveling) movement to self space (stationary) movement.
3. Have only half or even a third of the students participate in an activity with the rest of the class watching. Repeat the activity again with the other group(s) moving or rotate giving students a turn to participate on different days.
4. Assign students a choreographic structure and send small groups into hallways or other areas of the school building to create their dance or movement study.

Time Required

This heading gives you an approximate idea of how much time it will take to present the lesson. Lengths of the lessons in this book range between five and thirty-five minutes. Your actual presentation time may vary from the approximate time given depending on your personal teaching style and the responses of your students.

Introducing the Lesson

The lesson's introduction gives you and your students background information about the lesson's topic. Feel free to read the introduction to the students as it is written, paraphrase it, or write your own. The important thing is to be sure the students have a context for the activity they are about to engage in. Any words set in bold type in the introduction or body of the lesson can be found in the Glossary.

Teaching the Lesson

Although the lessons are written in a word-for-word scripted form, they are actually meant to be used as guides. They are written as scripts to show you one possible way of guiding the students through each lesson. Though you are welcome to read a lesson word-for-word it is hoped that you will adapt the manner of presentation to your teaching style and to the particular needs of your students.

Be aware as you teach the lessons that each question you pose or direction you give will elicit widely varying responses from your students. For example, if you ask "How could you use your body to show me rain falling from a cloud?" one student may respond by shaking many body parts, another may respond by repeatedly rising and falling and another might respond by creating raindrop sounds on the floor with her feet. All of these responses are valid, though they are very different. When guiding children in a movement activity your job is not to get them to respond "correctly," but to respond appropriately and creatively.

Another responsibility you have as a guide while students are exploring movement is to continually make them aware of possible choices. During any part of a lesson that asks you to allow the students time to explore an idea through movement, you can greatly aid your students by asking them questions based on the list of Movement Concepts and the partial listing of Locomotor and Non-Locomotor Movements, found on pages xii and xiii. Here are examples of the kinds of questions you might ask aloud as students are moving: "Could you try that movement on a different Level?...in a different Direction? ...Could you make the movement much larger?...much smaller?...Is it possible to change the Speed of the movement?"

Another way to encourage creative response as students are moving is to point out the interesting choices you see, for example: "Mary is really using her arms in a strong way! I see David turning as he floats. Joey and Rob are making a shape together." These kinds of statements not only acknowledge the students who are making creative choices; they also suggest new possibilities to the other students.

Concluding the Lesson

Each lesson concludes by asking students to review, in words, what they have learned during the movement portion of the lesson. In lessons involving choreography this review takes the form of evaluating the choreographic work of their peers. The conclusion of the lesson helps students integrate their right brain movement experience into their left brain as they verbalize the knowledge they have gained. It also helps you assess whether the lesson has been effective in teaching the content you wish to deliver. You may use the conclusion I suggest or design your own.

Troubleshooting

Sometimes, despite your best efforts, you may find yourself in the middle of a movement activity that seems "stuck": the students just don't know what to do. Before you panic and call a halt to the activity, try the following:

Give an example or demonstration of the kind of responses that you would like to see.

Simplify a complex lesson by only doing one part of it.

Do a choreographic activity as a whole class, with your guidance, rather than breaking the class into groups.

Let students know how they can get ideas when they feel stuck: look at the Movement Concepts chart, watch other students—in creative movement "copying" is great!

For more on managing movement activities, see "Managing Movement" on the following page.

Assessment

At some point after the lesson is completed, you will want to asses its effectiveness. I suggest waiting at least an hour or two before making an assessment because by that time you will be able to be more objective and less self-critical.

First, think about what went well in the lesson. When were the students particularly engaged? What were some really creative responses you observed? At what points did you feel that they really "got" the content of the lesson?

Next, take a look at any difficulties or problems you encountered and try to determine their cause. Were your directions to the students unclear? Did you neglect to direct the transitions from one part of the lesson to the next? Did you allow a student's negative behavior to garner too much of your attention? Being as specific as you can about the cause of any difficulties will help you avoid them in the future.

Last of all, just as you praise your students for striving for their highest potential, treat yourself well—no matter how the lesson went—for doing something that is new and challenging for you. You will find, over time, that using movement as a teaching tool seems less overwhelming and becomes, instead, vastly rewarding to both yourself and your students.

MANAGING MOVEMENT

When they imagine leading their students in a movement activity, many teachers envision a scene of noisy, directionless chaos. Unfortunately, the fear of such an occurrence often prevents these teachers from even attempting to use movement as a teaching tool. While a misdirected movement activity could certainly lead to noisy confusion, a well-planned, well executed lesson leads to engaged, motivated activity.

It is natural for a class to look and sound less controlled when engaging in movement than in some other educational processes. That is because the students are enthusiastic and excited and are actively involved with the content of the lesson and with each other. In other words, they're responding exactly the way we, as educators, should want them to respond. But because the standards for student behavior, formulated in a past generation, say that students are not learning unless they are sitting quietly at their desks, it is difficult for us to view this less controlled situation as a positive learning environment. We have to change our idea of what learning looks like in order to embrace movement as an appropriate educational activity.

Just as we must teach children the rules of a game before they can play it safely and successfully, we must educate them about *how* to engage in movement. In most classrooms, movement activities are not a part of the usual school day. There is no reason that students in such classrooms would know how to behave during a movement-based lesson. But often teachers who have never introduced movement before will try it once, then give up altogether because their students did not respond in the way they expected. This is as unfair to the students as it would be to give long division problems to a class that had never been introduced to long division, then say "never again" when they failed to solve the problems correctly!

This chapter will give you some general guidelines for leading your students in movement activities. Keep in mind, as you read, that "practice makes perfect" and the more you use movement as a teaching tool, the more positively and appropriately your students will respond.

Set clear expectations

As in any teaching situation, it is of vital importance to set clear boundaries and expectations for behavior. It is often helpful to have your students collaborate with you on creating a set of rules specifically for movement. An example of such a set of rules might be:

Listen and follow directions.
Move carefully, touch gently.
Make kind, positive comments.
Do excellent work.

It is best to state rules positively rather than telling students what they should not do. You may also want to set behavioral expectations specific to the space you are working in, such as "move only on the floor of the gym; stay off the bleachers." The clearer you can be at the outset about what kind of behavior you expect, the more safe your students will feel and the more positively they will respond.

It is useful to have a "freeze" signal; a signal which immediately stops all speaking and activity. A beat on a drum or tambourine works well for this purpose. It is a good idea to set up the freeze signal at the beginning of the very first movement activity you do with a group and to give the students a chance to practice responding to it several times.

Give clear directions

It is very possible for a movement activity to fail because directions were not given clearly. Giving clear directions means telling students exactly what they are expected to do. The Earth Science lessons in this book have been scripted so as to make the directions to students as clear as possible. It is important that students are always told where to go to begin a new activity and what to do when they get there. They need to be told how to engage in the activity and what to do when the activity has been completed.

The most common place for management to break down is in the transition between two sections of a lesson. For example, if the whole class does an improvisation and the students are then asked to get into groups to work on choreography, the transition from working as a class to working in groups could be problematic. It is important to plan exactly how the transition will take place and to communicate that plan to the students.

To get students into pairs or small groups, you may find it simplest to let them quickly make their own choices by giving them a task such as "by the time I count to ten, please find a friend (or two or three friends) and make a connected shape." Putting a time limitation on choosing groups prevents students from belaboring the process.

In some classes, due to interpersonal issues between students, asking them to choose their own partners or groups can be problematic. In this situation you may want to organize your students into appropriate groupings before beginning the lesson and read or post your list as part of preparing for an activity. Another possibility is to draw numbers out of a hat and allow groups to be chosen randomly.

Dividing your class in half can be accomplished simply by drawing an imaginary line through the middle of the group. Or, you may choose to have students "count off" 1's and 2's to make the grouping more random. The most important thing to remember in choosing groups is that it should happen quickly and matter-of-factly rather than becoming a major focus of the lesson.

Acknowledge appropriate behavior

One of the best ways to manage student behavior in any learning situation is to acknowledge appropriate behavior when you see it. It is just as important to praise positive behavior as it is to praise creativity. Your students yearn for your attention. Once they discover that behaving appropriately is the way to get that attention, they will eagerly exhibit the behavior you seek. Comments such as: "I really appreciate the way Billy is listening to my directions" or "Susan and Jesse are being very gentle with each other as they move together" let all of your students know what kind of behavior you value.

Acknowledging appropriate behavior is most effective when it is coupled with ignoring negative behavior. Although it can be extremely difficult to ignore a student who is behaving inappropriately it is crucial to successful classroom management. Try "catching" a difficult student behaving well—even for a second—and acknowledge him or her immediately.

Handling non-participation

A major concern for teachers who have never tried movement activities with their class is that their students "won't do it." My experience is that children of this age *love* to move and dance, and that most will gladly participate when given an opportunity. Boys, especially, are thrilled to have a chance to move when they discover that large, energetic movements are just as valued as graceful, delicate ones.

While most children participate in movement activities readily, it is not uncommon to have one or two students in a class who may initially resist joining in. Sometimes, if a child is timid or shy or comes from a family or cultural background where physical expression is not encouraged, he or she may feel threatened and overwhelmed when invited into a movement experience. It is usually best to let such students enter the activity when they feel ready. Allow them to watch for awhile so they can determine that the situation is physically, emotionally and socially safe. Most students who are initially timid will eventually participate eagerly.

Another type of non-participation stems from a student's desire to enter into a power struggle with you or to impress his or her peers by being too "cool" to participate. In this case it is best to simply state that participation is mandatory, just as it is for math or language arts. Your attitude carries a lot of weight in this situation: if *you* value movement as much as you value the other curricular subjects, your students are more likely to do so as well.

The bottom line in cases of non-participation is to use your good judgment and intuition to determine whether, in each individual situation, it is best to allow the child to be an observer or to ask him or her to rise to the challenge of full participation.

Managing the noise level

Students will naturally be more verbal when engaging in a movement activity than they are when sitting at their desks listening, reading or writing. It is important to determine whether the noise level is appropriate, as when they are talking with classmates to solve a movement problem, or when the noise level is higher than it needs to be. Many students have difficulty moving without speaking or making sounds because the only other time they have a chance to move is on the playground where shouting and yelling are the norm. They simply need training in how to move quietly.

I find it useful to demonstrate to the class that movement is a way to communicate and express oneself without sound. Ask them to show you, with their bodies, that they are excited...angry...sad...surprised. Encourage them to put the intensity of those feelings into their bodies without using their voices. Last of all, be sure to praise them whenever they are particularly successful in moving quietly.

Movement is motivating

Although you may find it challenging, initially, to manage movement activities with your class, over time you will find that movement becomes its own motivation. Your students will want to behave well because they will want you to keep providing them with movement experiences! Letting your students know that their involvement in movement is important to you is your most effective management tool.

INTRODUCTORY LESSONS

These two lessons will prepare students for the study of Earth Science by helping them understand some of the methods that scientists use to study the earth and the process of change on the earth itself. Lesson 1a introduces students to the use of observation, inference and hypothesis in doing science. Lesson 1b demonstrates the interconnectedness of all aspects of the earth, and how change in one part of the system eventually affects the entire planet.

Lesson 1a: Methods Used by Scientists

Topic:
Observation, Inference, Hypothesis, Experimentation

Type of Movement Activity:
Small Group Demonstration

Related Movement Concepts:
Place (self space, general space)

Materials / Preparation:
Before presenting this lesson gather a group of five or six students. Designate one student as the leader. Let the group know that they will be providing a demonstration for the rest of the class. When you say "go" they are to walk at a normal pace in the space cleared for the demonstration. When the leader stops they must all stop and remain frozen in position until the leader starts walking again. The leader should remain in position for at least ten slow counts—long enough that the observers are sure that everyone has stopped. It is important for other members of the group to also stop briefly at random times, but the only time *everyone* in the group will stop is when the leader stops.

Musical Suggestions:
No music required.

Space Requirements:
This lesson can easily take place in the regular classroom with a small amount of space cleared for the students who are providing the demonstration.

Time Required:
Approximately 15 minutes

Introduction:

Earth Science is the body of knowledge that has been discovered relating to our planet Earth. Though scientists use many different methods to make discoveries, there are some special things that most scientists do: they ***observe*** *or look closely at objects or events to discover* ***patterns****, things that occur repeatedly. When they notice a pattern they begin to make* ***inferences****, which are possible guesses as to why the pattern is taking place. Finally they state a* ***hypothesis****; a scientist's best guess about why something happens the way it does.*

Lesson:

I've asked a group of students to do a demonstration for you. Watch them carefully, and be ready to share what you observe.

(Have the group of five or six students perform the task you have outlined for them—see Materials / Preparation for this lesson. Let them continue the task for approximately two minutes, or until the leader has caused the group to stop at least three times.)

One of the most basic and important activities a scientist does is to observe, or look closely, at the world. Right now you are a scientist observing this event. What did you see? Don't try to explain why it happened, simply state what you observed.

(Students respond with observations.)

You just stated some simple observations about the demonstration you saw. Let's watch the demonstration again. This time be looking for any relationships you notice between events. In other words, does one event, such as a particular person stopping, seem to be connected to another event? Does one event appear to cause another?

(Have the small group repeat their demonstration. Guide the class in discussing any relationships they noticed.)

When scientists observe the world they look for patterns, or things that happen repeatedly. They also look for relationships between events, just as you have been doing. After noticing a pattern or relationship scientists begin to draw inferences, which means they think of possible explanations for what they've observed. What are some inferences we might draw about the event we've been observing? What might possibly be causing the whole group to stop at certain times?

(Students respond with possible explanations.)

When a scientist feels fairly sure that an inference is correct it becomes his or her hypothesis or "best guess" about why a pattern is occurring. Who can state their hypothesis about what causes everyone in the group to stop at the same time?

(Students respond with hypotheses. At this point many of them may have hypothesized that there is a leader who is causing the group to stop.)

How could we test our hypothesis to see if it is true?

(Students respond with possible tests. Repeat the demonstration using some tests that the students suggest. Someone will probably suggest trying the demonstration without particular group members participating in order to determine who is causing the group to stop.)

You have been using **experimentation** to test your hypotheses. After a scientist has tested a hypothesis many different times in various ways and found it to be consistently true, it can finally be stated as scientific **theory**, a hypothesis that is generally believed to be fact.

Conclusion:

As we begin our study of earth science it is important to keep in mind that all of the amazing knowledge we now have about the earth—from how volcanoes work to why the ocean has tides—began with someone observing the world, noticing a pattern, drawing inferences and formulating hypotheses to explain the cause of the pattern, then experimenting to test and strengthen their hypotheses. Our knowledge about the earth is constantly expanding as new patterns are observed. Perhaps someday you will observe an undiscovered pattern and develop a theory that gives people a new way of thinking about the world!

Variations:

You could add the element of scientific measurement to this lesson by having students record how many times the whole group stopped when various group members were removed from the demonstration. You might want to guide your students in creating a graph to display this data.

Extended Activities:

Ask students to read about a famous scientist such as Thomas Edison, Marie Curie, Alexander Graham Bell, etc. Ask individuals to report on an observation, an inference and a hypothesis made by that scientist, and how they tested their hypothesis.

Lesson 1b: The Earth is Always Changing

Topic:
Change, Interconnectedness

Type of Movement Activity:
Group Improvisational Exploration

Related Movement Concept:
Relationships (near, far, over, under, around, through)

Materials/ Preparation:
CD player or tape deck

Musical Suggestions:
Constant, dense (see Discography)

Space Requirements:
This lesson requires enough space for half of your class to stand fairly close together with a minimum amount of movement. Clearing a space at one end of the classroom by pushing desks against the walls would be adequate.

Time Required:
Approximately 10 minutes

Introduction:

The earth is always changing: rocks are changing into new types of rocks, material from inside the earth rises to the surface, water evaporates into the atmosphere, the oceans wear away the land. Every change in one part of the earth affects other parts of the earth. That is because everything on and around our planet is interconnected. Some forces, like volcanoes or earthquakes, may change the earth very quickly. But most of the changes on earth happen extremely slowly over hundreds, thousands, and even millions of years.

Lesson:

(Divide the class in half, asking half of the students to stand in the open space while half of them remain in their seats.)

Those of you who are standing will be creating a shape together, like a giant jigsaw puzzle. Move close together and find ways to be interconnected with the people around you by putting your whole body or parts of your body over, under, around or through the empty spaces that you see. You might imagine that your arm is a rainbow that reaches over someone. Or perhaps you are a rock nestled between two people. Maybe you are an icicle that reaches through the opening someone else has created. Once you've found a position you like, hold that position for a moment.

> *(Allow students a minute to create an interconnected shape.)*

When the music begins, I'm going to ask one person to make a small change in their shape. Perhaps that person will move their arm or leg, sink slowly to the floor, or press gently against someone else. Everyone needs to pay very close attention, and find a way to react to that change. Perhaps a movement of someone's arm will cause you to tip a little bit. Maybe as someone else sinks you will rise. Not everyone needs to react at the same time. If the change happens far away from you, you might wait until someone near you has reacted to the change, then react to them. Remember, things on earth change very slowly, so don't be afraid to let your reaction take a while to happen or to be very small. Once the whole group is still again, someone else can take the initiative to start a new change. Continue until I turn the music off.

> *(Choose one student to begin the sequence of change and reaction. If necessary, you may coach students by suggesting types of changes they could make: "Cindy, maybe you would sink to the floor when she touches you. Bob, you might twist when Peter leans against you" or asking a student to initiate a new change if the group gets "stuck." Continue for one to two minutes, then turn off the music. Ask this group of students to take their seats.)*

Before we let the other group take a turn, would anyone who was watching like to comment on what they saw? What examples of interconnectedness did you notice? Did you see any patterns in the way changes took place? Right now, you're doing what scientists do—looking for patterns and observing interconnections. Now let's give the second group a chance to create an interconnected shape.

> *(Repeat the activity with the other half of the class.)*

Conclusion:

You just had an experience of what "interconnectedness" means, and the kinds of cause and effect relationships that scientists look for when they observe changes on the earth.

Variations:

Instead of having half of the class work at a time, the whole class could work together in front of a video camera. The discussion would then take place after the film was played back.

Extended Activities:

Ask each student to write a short paragraph either describing their feelings during the activity, or describing what they observed in watching others do the activity. They might also write a paragraph about an example of how their own life is interconnected with the lives of others.

PART ONE

WHAT IS THE EARTH?

This group of lessons will deal with the various spheres that make up the structure of the earth. Lesson 2 will help students understand the inter relatedness of the earth's interior, lithosphere, hydrosphere, and atmosphere. Subsequent lessons will relate specifically to aspects of each sphere.

Lesson 2: Interrelated Spheres

Topic:
Interior, Lithosphere, Hydrosphere, Atmosphere

Type of Movement Activity:
Group Improvisational Exploration

Related Movement Concepts:
Weight (strong, light)
Energy (smooth, sharp)
Flow (free, bound)
Speed (slow, medium, fast)

Materials/ Preparation:
Your movement space will need to be divided into four areas, as shown on the next page. This can be done by taping the floor with painter's tape (easily removed), drawing lines with chalk, or laying down ropes.

Musical Suggestion:
Flowing (see Discography)

Space Requirements:
To have an entire class participate in this activity requires a large open space such as a gym, empty classroom, or outdoor area. A smaller group (six to eight students) could do this lesson as a demonstration in an open area of the classroom.

Time Required:
Approximately 10 minutes

Introduction:

The earth's structure can be thought of as having four divisions: the ***interior*** *or inside of the earth, the* ***lithosphere****—the solid land made of rocks and soil, the* ***hydrosphere****, which includes all of the water on earth, and the* ***atmosphere*** *or air that surrounds the earth.*

The energy and materials in these different parts of the earth are constantly being exchanged with each other. Material rises from the hot, molten interior of the earth and becomes part of the rocky crust. Pieces of the crust sink into the earth's interior. Soil from the lithosphere is carried into rivers and oceans of the hydrosphere. Oceans evaporate, and become clouds in the atmosphere.

Lesson:

Take a look at the divisions I've made on the floor. Each area represents one of the four divisions of the earth's structure. Together we're going to travel through each division to see what it's like; then we'll imagine that we're material and energy traveling freely between the divisions.

Let's begin in the interior of the earth. *(All students enter the "interior" area.)* This section is thick and molten, and is thought to have properties of both solids and liquids. Let's see how we might move if we were the dense, slowly flowing material inside the earth. Use your muscles to show how thick it is in the interior. Try pressing, pulling, squeezing movements. Try changing your level slowly as you move.

(Give students 20 to 30 seconds to explore movement that is flowing, yet thick and dense. This can be done with or without music.)

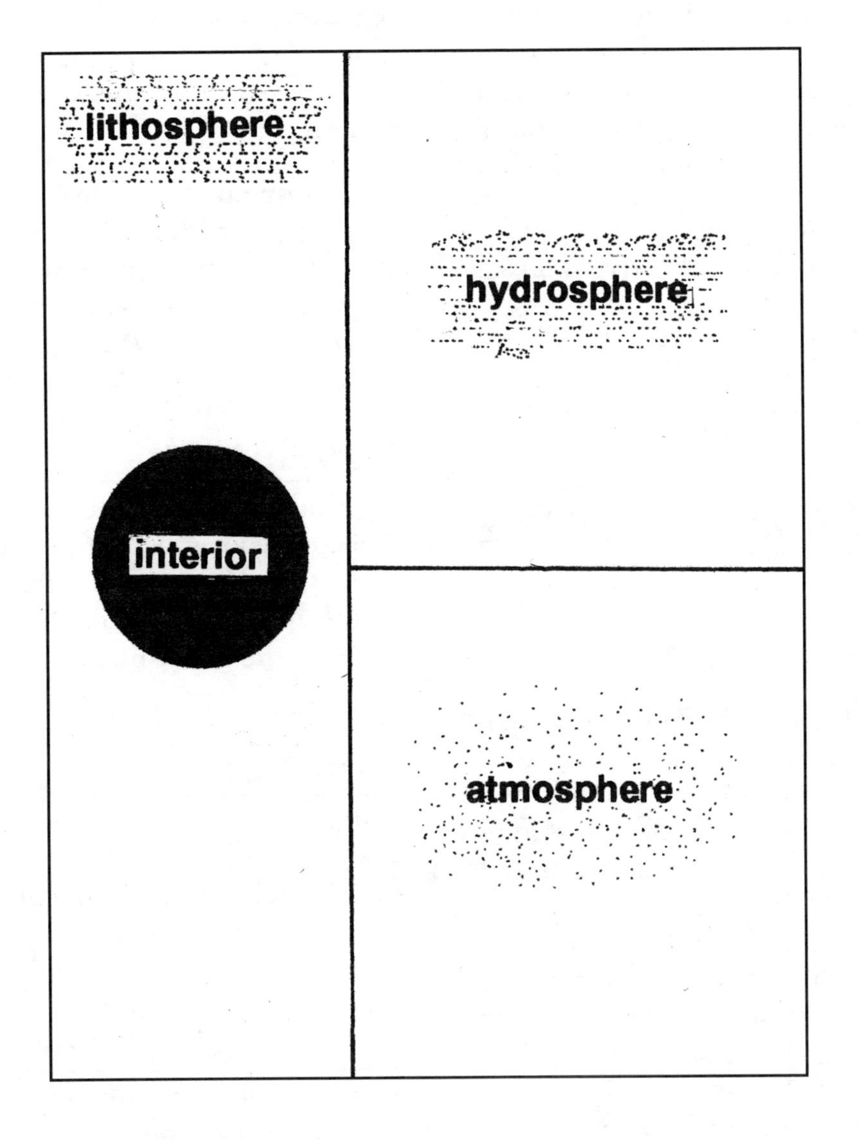

fig.1 Interrelated Spheres Floor Plan

Now let's all move to the lithosphere, which surrounds the interior. Here we have hard, solid material such as rocks, soil, and mountains. Experiment for a moment with making body shapes that are solid, hard, and still. How strong can you make your shape by tightening your muscles? Try some shapes that are sharp and angular like rocks, or shapes that are smooth and rounded like polished stones.

(Allow students 20 to 30 seconds to explore making rigid body shapes.)

Next we'll move to the hydrosphere. Here the material is liquid—it flows freely. Take a minute to move as a liquid in the hydrosphere. How would your arms move if you were made of liquid? Your head? Your back? Maybe your liquid would flow backwards or sideways.

(Allow students 20 to 30 seconds to explore flowing, "watery" movement.)

Last of all, let's all spread out into the atmosphere. The material here is gaseous—it's light and airy, with **molecules**—tiny, invisible particles—that are far apart like we are now. Take a moment to imagine that you're a molecule floating through the atmosphere. Relax your muscles and see how lightly you can float, turn or skip. Try some light movements that are very large and some that are tiny.

(Allow students 20 to 30 seconds to explore light, floating movements.)

Now, by the time I count to ten, I'd like each person to choose a division to go to and make a shape with their body.

When the music begins you may move freely in your division. Remember what the material there is made of, and what type of movement you did there. At any time you may switch to another division, but you must also change your way of moving as you enter the new division. When I stop the music, freeze wherever you are.

(Allow students one to three minutes to move freely between the divisions. Guide them by reminding them of the types of movements they might do in each division. Turn music off.)

Conclusion:

Let's take a quick vote to find out which division you most enjoyed moving in. Raise your hand if you enjoyed the interior the most...the lithosphere...the hydrosphere...the atmosphere.

Variation:

Instead of having the students move at any time between areas, you could use a signal such as a drumbeat to tell them when to move to another area.

Extended Activities:

Provide students with textured materials such as sandpaper, cotton, velvet, and clay. Have them use the idea of interior, lithosphere, hydrosphere and atmosphere in creating a texture collage.

Section A: Earth's Interior

We live on the lithosphere, the solid part of the earth made of rock and soil. But the lithosphere is only a thin crust on the sphere that is the earth. When compared with the thickness of the whole planet, the lithosphere is like the skin of an apple.

Below the lithosphere lies the mantle. Some scientists believe that the mantle is divided into several layers. The mantle moves slowly and is probably the consistency of thick sludge or putty.

Inside the mantle is the earth's outer core. The outer core contains liquid iron and nickel. Interior even to this layer is the inner core, which is extremely hot and under great pressure.

Lesson 3: Core, Mantel, Crust

Topic:
Core, Mantle, Crust

Type of Movement Activity:
Group Improvisational Exploration

Related Movement Concepts:
Weight: (strong, light)
Flow: (free, bound)

Materials/ Preparation:
CD or tape player (optional)

Musical Suggestions:
Constant, dense (see Discography)

Space Requirements:
Adequate space for your entire class to stand fairly close to one another with a moderate amount of movement. An empty classroom, half of a gym or lunchroom, a stage area or an outdoor space would be optimal. To adapt this lesson for the regular classroom have all students do each of the movements described in self space (not traveling) while standing behind their chairs.

Time Required:
Approximately 10 minutes

Introduction:

If we were to journey four thousand miles down from the outer crust of the earth, where we live, we would come to the earth's ***inner core.*** *The inner core is extremely hot—about 8,100 degrees Fahrenheit! The material here is under tremendous pressure—about 24,000 tons of pressure per square inch.*

Surrounding the earth's inner core is the ***outer core,*** *which is about 13,000 miles thick. The outer core is made of molten iron, nickel and oxygen. These materials are in a liquid form which flows very slowly.*

Surrounding the earth's outer core is a layer called the ***mantle,*** *which is over 1,700 miles thick. The mantle is the consistency of thick sludge or putty. It flows very slowly, carrying continents as it moves.*

*The very surface layer of the earth is called the **crust**. It is only three to twenty miles thick, and is made of solid rock and soil. Compared to the thickness of the earth's interior, the crust is like the skin of an apple.*

Lesson:

We're going to create a model of the earth's interior in this space, using our bodies. First I need four or five people to come to the center of the space and be the inner core. Remember, there is great pressure in the inner core. How will you show that pressure with your bodies? Try pressing or pushing against the space with your arms, legs, heads and backs. Try squeezing and stretching with lots of strength.

It is also very hot in the inner core. How might you show this? Might you shake some of your body parts or flick, poke or dab sharply? Will you move your body quickly or slowly to show the heat in the inner core?

> *(Ask the inner core students to remain in place but relax for a moment while you work to establish the outer core.)*

Now I need seven or eight people to be the outer core. Let's have these people surround the inner core. Remember, the outer core is molten, liquid rock which flows slowly. How will you show this, outer core? What body parts can you move slowly. Which direction will you travel? Might you change your level as you flow slowly around the inner core?

Now let's see the inner and outer cores moving at the same time.

> *(Ask the inner and outer core students to remain in place and relax for a moment while you work to establish the mantle.)*

Now I need nine or ten people to be the mantle. *(Note: Numbers of students in each section will vary with the size of your class. The mantle should have the largest number of students.)* Mantle, you have the consistency of sludge or putty, moving extremely slowly around the outer core. How will you show this in movement? We should really see your muscles working as you move. Will you walk...turn...roll...slide?

Now let's see the inner core, outer core and mantle moving at the same time.

> *(Ask the inner core, outer core and mantle students to remain in place and relax while you work to establish the crust.)*

Last of all we need to add the crust to our model. I'd like all of you who are not part of the inner core, outer core or mantle to come up and form a circle around the mantle. Remember, the crust is rigid and solid. Please show this with your bodies. You'll need to really tighten your muscles to show us how solid the crust is. Will you make shapes that are straight...curved... angular...twisted? Is there a way that some pieces of the crust could be carried along by the slow movement of the mantle?

Now let's put all of these movements together, and see what the interior of our earth is like. *(Music during this is helpful, but optional.)*

Conclusion:

Think for a moment about what you learned today about the interior of the earth. Did you learn anything that surprised you?

Variations:

Rather than having the group work as a whole, the class could be divided into four groups: inner core, outer core, mantle, and crust. Each group could work for five minutes on its own to develop a group movement before putting all the groups together.

Extended Activities:

Ask students to write a short story about a journey to the center of the earth. They must use some vocabulary and facts from the lesson, but they can add imaginary events or characters.

Section B: The Lithosphere

In the next section of lessons, the students will be learning about the part of the earth upon which we live: the lithosphere. The lithosphere is the solid part of the earth that is made of rocks and soil. Our study of the lithosphere will include a look at the states and properties of matter, the properties of minerals, and the different types of rocks and how they are formed.

UNIT 1: MATTER

Matter is anything that occupies space and has mass. All matter is made up of tiny particles called molecules. The organization of these molecules tells us whether the matter is in a solid, liquid, or gaseous state.

All matter can be described in terms of its properties, which include color, size, weight, taste, shape, texture and smell.

Some kinds of matter are made up of only one type of atom, and are called elements. A compound is a substance that is made up of two or more elements joined together. A mixture is made up of two or more elements or compounds which can be separated into parts.

The lessons in this unit provide movement experiences to help students understand the states, properties and organization of matter.

Lesson 4: States of Matter

(This lesson is based on a dance activity developed by Anne Green Gilbert)

Topic:
Solid, Liquid, Gas

Type of Movement Activity:
Group Improvisational Exploration
Small Group Choreography

Related Movement Concepts:
Relationships (near, far, over, under, around, through)
Size (big, medium, little)
Flow (free, bound)

Materials/Preparation:
CD player or tape deck

3x5 cards or small pieces of paper (1 for every five or six students). Each card should have three words written on it, one representing a solid, one a liquid, and one a gas. Make sure there is a sense of logical connection between the three words.

Examples:

ice cube (solid)
water (liquid)
steam (gas)

steam (gas)
lava (liquid)
hardened lava (solid)

iceberg (solid)
ocean (liquid)
water vapor (gas)

Musical Suggestions:
Constant, dense or flowing (see Discography)

Space Requirements: This activity requires enough space for the entire class to move freely, as well as for small groups to work simultaneously. An empty classroom, gym, stage, or outdoor space would be optimal. The beginning of the lesson can also be done as a small group demonstration at the front of the regular classroom. For the choreography portion of the lesson, groups of students could work in different areas of the classroom or in a hallway if appropriate, then show their finished work at the front of the classroom.

Time Required:
Approximately 25 minutes

Introduction:

Matter *is anything that takes up space and has* ***mass****, or substance. Most of what you see in the world is matter. What you can't see are molecules, the tiny particles that make up all matter. Depending on how these molecules are arranged, matter can be in one of three states:* ***solid****,* ***liquid*** *or* ***gas****. The molecules in a solid are close together and move very little. In a liquid, molecules are farther apart and move more freely. Molecules are farthest apart and show the most movement in a gas.*

Lesson:

First we're all going to imagine that we are molecules in something that is solid. Who can give us an example of a substance on earth that is solid? *(Appropriate responses could include rock, wood, ice, etc.)* The molecules in a solid are very close together, so let's all come together in this small space in the corner of the room. Molecules in a solid move, but they are so close together that their movement is very small and controlled. Try doing tiny movement with your arms...legs...and heads. Can you move around the other molecules by taking extremely small steps?

(Allow students 20 to 30 seconds to explore moving slightly as they stay tightly packed together in a small amount of space. Music here is optional, but helpful.)

Next we're going to see what it's like to be molecules in a liquid. Someone please name a liquid that is found on earth. *(Appropriate responses include water, lava, sap, etc.)* The molecules in a liquid are farther apart than in a solid, so let's spread out a bit more in the space. As a liquid, we can use half of the room to move in. Because you have more room to move in, you will probably notice that your movements can be larger and more free-flowing. You might find yourself stretching, swirling or swaying.

(Allow students 20 to 30 seconds to explore moving as a liquid in half of the movement space.)

Last of all, let's imagine that we're a gas such as steam, smoke or water vapor. The molecules in a gas are much farther apart, so we can spread out and use the whole space. Now you will have room to do movements that are very large and free. Try floating, leaping or rolling freely.

(Allow students 20 to 30 seconds to explore moving as a gas, using the entire space.)

Now that you've had a chance to move as molecules in a solid, a liquid and a gas, I'm going to give you a chance to choreograph your own movement studies about states of matter. When you choreograph, you plan the movements that you and your group will do before you do them.

In a moment I will divide the class into groups of five or six. I will give each group a card that has three words on it: one word is a solid, one is a liquid, one is a gas—but they're not necessarily in that order. With your group, you need to plan movement to show how your solid turns into a liquid, then into a gas—or whatever order is on your card. Show us how and why the changes happen—do they happen slowly? Quickly? Is there something that is *not* on your card that causes the change to happen? For example, is it the sun that melts your ice cube, or a volcano exploding that causes liquid lava to flow? You may want to show the cause of the changes, as well as the changes themselves.

You will have about ten minutes to plan your movement study. Be sure it has a beginning and an end. Once you have planned your study, practice it two times to make sure you know it.

(Divide the students into groups of five or six, and give each group a card. Allow the groups to work independently for six to ten minutes. It is helpful to circulate among the groups as they work, clarifying directions and solving problems.)

Now we'll perform our movement studies for each other. I expect you to show your respect for your classmates as they perform by watching quietly, and applauding when they are finished.

(Allow each group an opportunity to perform their study. Music is helpful in providing motivation and decreasing self-consciousness.)

Conclusion:

After each group's performance, allow the audience to respond to the following questions:

Could you clearly see a solid, a liquid and a gas in the study?

Can you guess what this group's three words might have been?

How did this group show the changes in the states of matter?

What one part of the study most caught your attention?

Variations:

Instead of having several individual choreographic assignments, you could give one assignment to the entire class. For example, ask the class to show how an ice cube becomes water which then becomes steam. Divide the class into three groups—one is the ice cube, one the water, and one the steam. Each group would create its own movement, but the whole class would have to plan the transitions between each group's "turn" to move.

Extended Activities:

Ask students to notice solids, liquids and gases as they go through their daily lives. Ask them to keep a list for several days of substances they notice in these three states. Create a classroom chart listing all the examples collected by the students.

Lesson 5: Properties of Matter

Topic:
Color, Size, Weight, Taste, Shape, Texture, Smell, State

Type of Movement Activity:
Group Improvisational Exploration
Small Group Choreography

Related Movement Concepts:
Size (big, medium, little)
Energy (smooth, sharp)
Weight (strong, light)
Shape (straight, curved, angular, twisted)
Flow (free, bound)

Materials / Preparation:
CD player or tape deck

Small samples of various substances, which could include salt, sugar, water, oil, apple, wood, clay, etc.

Blackboard and chalk or chart paper and felt pen

Pencil and one sheet of paper for each group of five or six students

Musical Suggestions:
Any selection from Discography

Space Requirements:
This activity requires adequate space for the entire class to move freely, and for small groups to work simultaneously. An empty classroom, gym, stage or outdoor area would be optimal. In a regular classroom ask students to stand behind their desks and do movements in self space (not traveling). The choreography section of the lesson could be done with small groups working in different areas of the room, then showing their finished work at the front of the classroom.

Time Required:
Approximately 25 minutes

Introduction:

*Scientists who study the earth describe **properties** of matter. Matter is anything that takes up space and has mass. Properties are characteristics that help us identify matter, and distinguish one substance from another. The properties of matter are: color, size, weight, taste, shape, texture, smell and state.*

Lesson:

I have in my hand a substance that all of you are familiar with: common table salt. Let's describe the properties of salt in words; then we'll try describing them through movement.

(Using the blackboard or chart paper, write one or two word descriptions of the color, size, weight, taste, shape, texture, smell and state of salt, as decided upon by the class.)

Example:
Color: white
Size: tiny grains
Weight: light
Taste: salty
Shape: crystals
Texture: grains
Smell: none
State: solid

Now let's go through our list and see if we can come up with a movement that describes each of these properties. We'll start with Color: white. It's difficult to think of color as having a movement, but let's think about it for a moment. If you imagine the color white, does it make you want to move fast or slow? Smoothly or sharply? Does it make you feel like floating? Pressing? Swinging? I'll give each of you a moment to come up with your own movement that you feel describes the color white. There is no right or wrong answer.

(Allow students 20 to 30 seconds to come up with a movement for "white." Every student will interpret the color differently. Music is optional, but helpful.)

Let's take a look at the many ways you thought of to describe the color white through movement. When I turn on the music, I'd like half of the class to show the movement they created.

(Quickly divide the group in half, asking half of the students to perform their movement while the other half sits and watches. Then reverse roles.)

Now we'll move on to the next property of salt, which is its size.

(Repeat the preceding process for the other properties of salt. It's very helpful to refer students to the Movement Concepts (see chapter "What Are Movement Concepts?") to help them create movements. Do this by asking questions such as: "Does the taste of salt make you want to move quickly or slowly?" "Are the shapes of salt crystals curved or angular?" "Is the texture of salt smooth or sharp?" Having a list of the Movement Concepts as well as some Locomotor and Non-Locomotor Movements posted in the room is also highly recommended.)

Now that you see how it's possible to describe the properties of a substance through movement, I'm going to give you some other substances to describe. In a moment I'll divide you into small groups and give each group a sample of a substance. First I'd like you to list all the properties of the substance on a piece of paper, using the list on the board as a guide. Then decide as a group how to show those properties in movement.

(Divide the class into groups of five or six and give each group a sample of a substance, a pencil and a sheet of paper. Circulate among the groups, giving assistance and direction as needed.)

Now, let's watch the movement of each group as they describe their substance.

(Allow each group an opportunity to perform. You may let the group choose whether or not they wish to perform with music.)

Conclusion:

After each group's performance, allow the audience to respond to the following questions:

Would anyone like to guess what substance this group was describing?

Which property of the substance did the group show most clearly?

What Movement Concepts did this group use to describe their substance?

Variations:

Instead of using background music, ask the group to create a sound to go along with each movement. The sounds could be vocal sounds or body sounds such as clapping, stomping or slapping.

Extended Activities:

Ask individual students or groups to describe properties of a substance of their choice using one of the following: a drawing or collage, sound or music, a poem.

Lesson 6: Elements, Compounds & Mixtures

Topic:
Elements, Compounds and Mixtures

Type of Movement Activity:
Group Shape

Related Movement Concepts:
Shape (straight, curved, angular, twisted)
Relationship (near, far, over, under, around, through)

Materials / Preparation:
None

Musical Suggestions:
No music required

Space Requirements:
This activity involves a minimal amount of movement, and can be done in one area of the regular classroom with some desks pushed aside.

Time Required:
Approximately 10 minutes

Introduction:

*All matter is thought to be made up of incredibly small particles called **atoms**. These particles are too small to be seen, even with a microscope. Some substances, called **elements**, contain only one type of atom. The atoms in an element contain all the physical properties of that element.*

*Many elements on the earth are combined with at least one other element to make a new substance called a **compound**. Compounds that are found as natural solids within the earth's crust are called **minerals**.*

*When two or more elements or compounds are found together and can be separated easily into their component parts they are called a **mixture**. Soil is an example of a mixture.*

Lesson:

In order to do our activity today, you need to know a little about the four kinds of shapes your body can make. Everyone please stand up right behind your chair, and try these shapes with me.

Straight shapes are shapes that are completely stretched, with no bends or angles in them. Try a straight shape with your arm...your leg...your entire body. Show me another straight shape.

A curved shape is rounded and smooth like a circle or the letter C. Show me a curved shape with your arm...your back... your whole body. Try one more curved shape.

An angular shape bends at the joints—elbows, knees, hips, wrists and ankles. Show me an angular arm shape...an angular leg shape...a body shape with many angles in it...and another.

A twisted shape twists and spirals around itself. It might make you think of a pretzel or a knot. Try a twisted shape with your body...and another twisted shape.

Now, I'd like to have five students come to the front of the room. These five students are going to represent atoms in an element. Remember that all of the atoms in an element are the same, and that they contain all the properties of that element. To simplify things, let's represent "all the properties" of this element as a shape. Let's make this an element in which all of the atoms are straight shapes.

> *(Guide the five students to stand close together in straight shapes.)*

Now I need another five students to form a different element. Would you please form an element in which all of the atoms are curved shapes.

> *(Guide the second five students to stand close together in curved shapes.*

What would need to happen in order for these two elements to form a compound? That's right—they'd have to join together. And remember, it's very difficult to separate the elements in a compound. How might these students show that? Yes, maybe they could actually hook their straight and curved shapes together so they can't be separated.

(Guide students in creating a group shape in which the five straight shapes are linked with the five curved shapes.)

You've created a great example of a compound. Now we're going to put two elements together in a different way to form a mixture. Could I please have five students come up and form an element in which all of the atoms are angular shapes.

Now I need another element in which all of the atoms are twisted shapes. Everyone who has not yet had a turn please come up and be a part of this "twisted shape" element.

How will we turn these two elements into a mixture? Does anyone remember how a mixture is different from a compound? That's right—the elements in a mixture can be more easily separated. How could we show that?

(Allow students to discover a solution. Perhaps the twisted and angular shapes will intermingle, yet have spaces between them.)

Conclusion:

Let's take a moment to review what you've just learned. Who can tell me what an element is? What is the difference between an element and a compound? Between a compound and a mixture?

Variations:

Instead of using the Movement Concept "Shapes" to do this demonstration, try using another concept such as Levels. The elements then would consist of High, Medium or Low atoms which would then join together to create compounds and mixtures.

Extended Activities:

Ask students to imagine that they need to draw a diagram or pictograph that explains, to someone who can't read, the difference between an element, a compound and a mixture.

UNIT 2: MINERALS

A mineral is a naturally occurring substance found in the earth's crust and upper mantle, consisting of a single compound. (Sometimes minerals may consist of a single element, but this is very rare.) Although minerals are very different from each other, they all have four things in common:

1. All minerals are combinations of certain key elements.
2. All minerals are found in nature; not made by humans.
3. All minerals are inorganic—they are not made by or from living things.
4. All minerals are crystalline solids—their atoms are locked into fixed, repeating patterns.

Like all matter, minerals are identified according to certain physical properties. In the case of minerals, these properties are cleavage, fracture, hardness, color, streak and luster.

Lesson 7: Properties of Minerals

Topic:
Cleavage, Fracture, Hardness, Streak

Type of Movement Activity:
Partner Improvisational Exploration

Related Movement Concepts:
Shape (straight, curved, angular, twisted)
Direction (forward, backward, sideways, up, down)
Weight (strong, light)

Materials / Preparation:
Photographs or illustrations (see opposite page) of various mineral specimens showing examples of cleavage and fracture (optional but extremely helpful). Such photographs can be found in many Earth Science textbooks and in books about minerals and gems.

Musical Suggestions:
No music required

Space Requirements: This activity involves a minimal amount of movement and could be done in the aisles of a regular classroom or in an open space such as a gym.

Time Required:
Approximately 10 minutes

Introduction:

*A mineral is a natural substance found in the earth's crust and upper mantle which consists of a single compound or element. Some minerals you may be familiar with are quartz, garnet and mica, but there are many others. The scientists who study minerals are called **geologists**. Geologists identify minerals by looking at certain of their properties such as the mineral's **cleavage** or ability to break into smooth, parallel surfaces, its **fracture** or tendency to break in other ways, its **hardness** or ability to resist scratching and its **streak** or tendency to leave traces of color behind when rubbed on a smooth surface.*

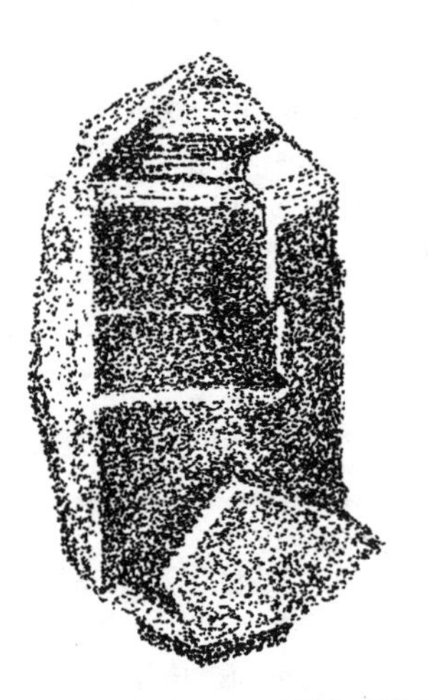

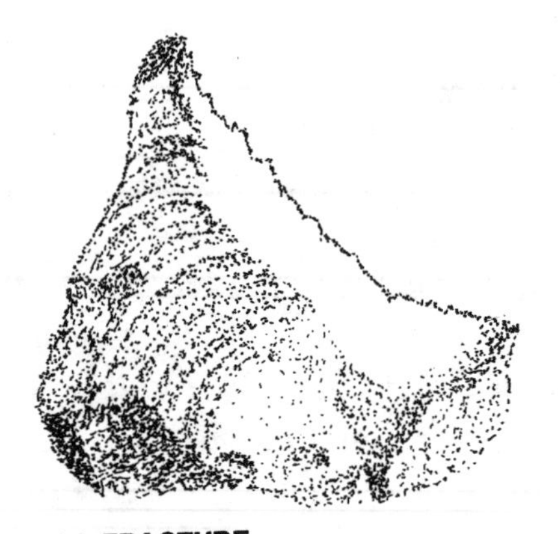

fig. 2 Cleavage and Fracture of Minerals

Lesson:

(Organize students into pairs. If there is an extra student ask him or her to work with you or to join another pair and form a trio. Assign one person in each pair to be the geologist and one to be the mineral.)

Let's learn about one of the properties a geologist looks for when identifying a mineral—cleavage. Cleavage is the ability of a mineral to break into smooth, parallel surfaces. Some minerals break into just one flat surface; others break into several surfaces that lie in different directions. *(Showing a photograph or illustration of a mineral with cleavage breaks would be helpful here.)*

Take a moment with your partner and decide how you will show the geologist breaking a mineral. You must think of a way to do this where the geologist does not actually touch the mineral. Perhaps the geologist will use one of his or her body parts to slash the air.

Mineral, decide if you will break into one or several flat surfaces and how you will show those surfaces with your body. Perhaps you'll make a shape lying on the floor with your legs reaching in one direction and your arms reaching in two different directions.

Now, let's watch and see how several pairs solved the problem of showing a geologist breaking a mineral into several cleavage directions. *(Allow several pairs to perform their movements for the class.)*

Next, let's look at another way minerals can break, called fracture. Minerals that fracture don't have cleavage, but break in other ways. An example of a fracturing mineral is quartz, which breaks into curved, rounded surfaces. *(Showing a photograph or illustration of broken quartz would be helpful here.)*

Let's switch roles this time—the person who was the mineral last time will be a geologist breaking a piece of quartz. Remember that you cannot actually touch your partner as you do this. The person who was the geologist last time will be a piece of quartz fracturing along a curved surface. Please take a moment to decide how you will show this. Will you create a shape where your back is curved and rounded...your arms...your legs?

Now let's watch some new pairs, and see how they show a geologist testing for the property of fracture.

(Allow several new pairs to perform their movement for the class.)

Let's take a look at another mineral property—hardness. Geologists test minerals for hardness by scratching them with a second mineral. The mineral that can scratch the other is the hardest. There are ten special minerals that are used to test hardness, but you can also do an informal test by scratching a mineral with your fingernail, a copper penny and an iron nail.

Switch roles again, and decide how you will show a geologist testing a mineral for hardness. The geologist might imagine that he or she is holding a mineral to test with, or that person might choose to actually *be* several minerals scratching the first mineral. Please do not actually touch each other as you do this. Take a moment to decide how you will show a test for hardness. What body parts might the geologist use to scratch the mineral?

Let's watch a few pairs show their test for hardness.

(Allow several pairs to perform their movement for the class.)

One of the first things that a geologist might notice about a mineral is its color, but color is not considered very helpful in identifying a mineral because many minerals can be of a similar color. Instead, geologists use a property called streak. Streak is tested by rubbing a mineral against a flat piece of unglazed porcelain. Minerals that are softer than the porcelain will leave a streak of color behind.

Switching roles again, show how a mineral is tested for streak. Like last time, the geologist can rub the mineral against an imaginary piece of porcelain, or might actually choose to play the part of the porcelain. How will you show the streak? Will the mineral stretch one of his or her arms or legs along the floor to represent the streak?

Who would like to show their mineral being tested for streak? *(Allow several pairs to perform their movement for the class.)*

Conclusion:

Today we've learned about some of the properties a geologist looks at in identifying a mineral. To review, I'll name each property that we learned about one more time. As I name it, see if you can remember and repeat the movement you created with your partner: Cleavage...fracture... hardness...streak.

Variations:

After doing this exercise in partners, the class could be broken into small groups. Each group would choose the test for one mineral property and show it in movement. The rest of the class would try to guess which property the pair is showing.

Extended Activities:

Obtain samples of some common minerals and allow students to test them for some of the properties they've studied. Two other properties that can be observed are crystal faces—the smooth, flat surfaces of crystals, and heft—the weight of a mineral.

UNIT 3: ROCKS

The surface of the earth contains an abundant amount of a mixture of minerals called rock. Besides the rocks we can easily see, there is solid rock underneath the soil, and rocks underneath the oceans.

Rocks are divided into three major classes:

1. Igneous rock, which is formed from magma—the melted rock beneath the earth's surface.
2. Sedimentary rock, which is formed from particles of other rocks and minerals or remains of living organisms that have been deposited in one place and pressed into layers.
3. Metamorphic rock, which has been changed from one type of rock to another by heat and pressure.

All rocks constantly change from one class to another through a process called the rock cycle.

Lesson 8: Classes of Rock

Topic:
Igneous, Sedimentary and Metamorphic Rock

Type of Movement Activity:
Group Improvisational Exploration

Related Movement Concepts:
Flow (free, bound)
Weight (strong, light)
Relationship (near, far, over, under, around, through)

Materials / Preparation:
CD player or tape deck

hand drum

Musical Suggestions:
Igneous rock: "Lucky Stiff," *Music for Creative Dance: Contrast and Continuum Volume I,* Eric Chappelle, or Flowing (see Discography)

Sedimentary Rock: Constant, dense (see Discography)

Metamorphic Rock: Constant, dense (see Discography)

Space Requirements:
This activity requires adequate space for the entire class to move freely, such as a gym, empty classroom, stage or outdoor space. To do this lesson in the regular classroom ask students to stand behind their chairs and do the movements for "igneous rock" with minimal traveling. The sections on sedimentary and metamorphic rock could be done as smaller group demonstrations at the front of the classroom.

Time Required:
Approximately 10 minutes

Introduction:

All of the rocks in and on the earth are divided into three major classes according to how they are formed. The names of these classes are ***igneous, sedimentary*** *and* ***metamorphic*** *rock.*

Lesson:

We'll begin by learning about igneous rock. Igneous, which comes from the Latin word "ignus" or fire, is the name for rock which is formed from molten magma from under the earth. The hot magma flows, then cools and crystallizes into rocks. Sometimes the magma flows to the surface as lava before it cools.

When the music begins we're all going to imagine that we're magma or lava flowing freely. We'll keep our bodies moving without stopping. When you hear the music change and become stiffer and sharper, let your movement start to become more controlled as if you are cooling and crystallizing. Finally, stop and form a rock shape, either alone or with someone else. When the music begins to flow smoothly again, let your rock melt and become magma or lava once more.

(Note: This activity was specifically designed to be performed to the selection listed under "Musical Suggestions" above. If you do not have access to this selection, play any Flowing selection (see Discography), then turn it off and beat a drum as the "rocks" are cooling.)

> *(Allow students to explore flowing and cooling while guiding them with suggestions such as: "Could you do*

flowing movements with your arms? Your back? Might your magma flow in a curved or zig-zag pathway? What type of shapes will your body make as you turn into a rock? Will you change your level?)

Now we'll take a look at a class of rock which forms very differently—sedimentary rock. The word sedimentary comes from a Latin word which means "to settle." When rocks get broken up by rain, running water, earthquakes or wind they form small pieces of rock called **sediments.** These sediments are carried—usually by moving water—and deposited in one place. Layer upon layer of particles build up and press against each other. Certain elements in the water form a cement that joins the particles of sediment together until they are solid rock.

So that no one gets hurt, we are going to form our layers of sediment using only our arms.

When the music begins you may all move freely around the room as if you are particles of rock and minerals being carried by water. As you move, I will call out five people's names. As I call their names, those five people will come to the center of the room and stop moving. They will hold out their arms and layer them on top of each other, imagining that their arms are sediment settling to the bottom of a river. Then I will call another five names, and the five new people will settle their arms on top of the first five. Please remain standing and settle your arms very gently, so no one will be hurt.

(Turn on music. Call out names five at a time, and guide the students in coming to the center and "settling" their arms in layers. You may want the students to form several groups to minimize crowding. When all have joined a group turn music off.)

Now let's imagine that lots of time has gone by, and these layers have become cemented together into one solid rock. See if you can find a way to join the layers so they are all connected. Perhaps you'll intertwine your arms, or tighten your muscles to make your arms like a solid rock.

The final class of rock we'll learn about today is metamorphic rock. As you may know, **metamorphosis** is the process of changing from one form to another, which is exactly what these rocks do. Heat and pressure causes changes in the atoms that make up the minerals in a rock. The rocks may also bend or fold into layers due to pressure.

(Divide the class in half, asking half of the students to come to the center of the room.)

I'd like you to imagine that you are the atoms in a piece of metamorphic rock, and make a large shape together. Think about how you can relate to the other atoms in the shape—some key words to remember are "over, under, around and through." Try reaching your arm over another person...putting your legs under someone's shape...curving your body around someone else...stretching a body part through an open space.

The rest of us are going to be the heat and pressure that acts upon the metamorphic rock. We'll start at the edges of the room and move slowly toward the shape in the center, imagining that we're pushing inward with very strong pressure. People in the center, see if you can slowly change your shape, level or position as we press toward you. We'll stop when I call out "freeze," before we actually touch anyone. Please find your places at the edge of the room and begin pressing when I turn on the music.

(Turn music on. Allow students on the edges to press toward the shape in the center. Call out "freeze" when the pressers are about a foot away from the shape.)

Great—look how much the shape in the center has changed! Do you see any bends or folds in the rock?

(Repeat the activity so that the other group gets a chance to be the metamorphic rock.)

Conclusion:

We just learned a little about how each of the three major classes of rock are formed. Who would like to tell me which type of rock was most interesting to be a part of, and why?

Variations:

Instead of doing this activity as lecture / demonstration for the entire class, you could assign one of the classes of rock to each of three groups, and ask them to choreograph movement to show the formation of their rock type.

Extended Activities:

Have students choose one of the classes of rock, and write a short story about the adventures of a particle of that rock as it is being formed.

Lesson 9: The Rock Cycle

Topic:
The Rock Cycle

Type of Movement Activity:
Individual Improvisational Exploration
Small Group Choreography

Related Movement Concepts:
Shape (straight, curved, angular, twisted)
Size (big, medium, little)
Levels (high, middle, low)
Weight (strong, light)
Flow (free, bound)

Materials / Preparation:
Large diagram of the rock cycle on a blackboard or butcher paper (see next page)

CD player or tape deck (optional)

3x5 cards (one for every 4-6 students), each showing one portion of the rock cycle (see examples on page 29)

Musical Suggestions:
Constant, dense (see Discography)

Space Requirements:
This lesson would optimally take place in a space large enough for students to move freely such as a gym, empty classroom, stage or outdoor area. However, it would also be possible to do in a regular classroom if all of the movements were done in self space (in one place, without traveling).

Time Required:
Approximately 25 minutes

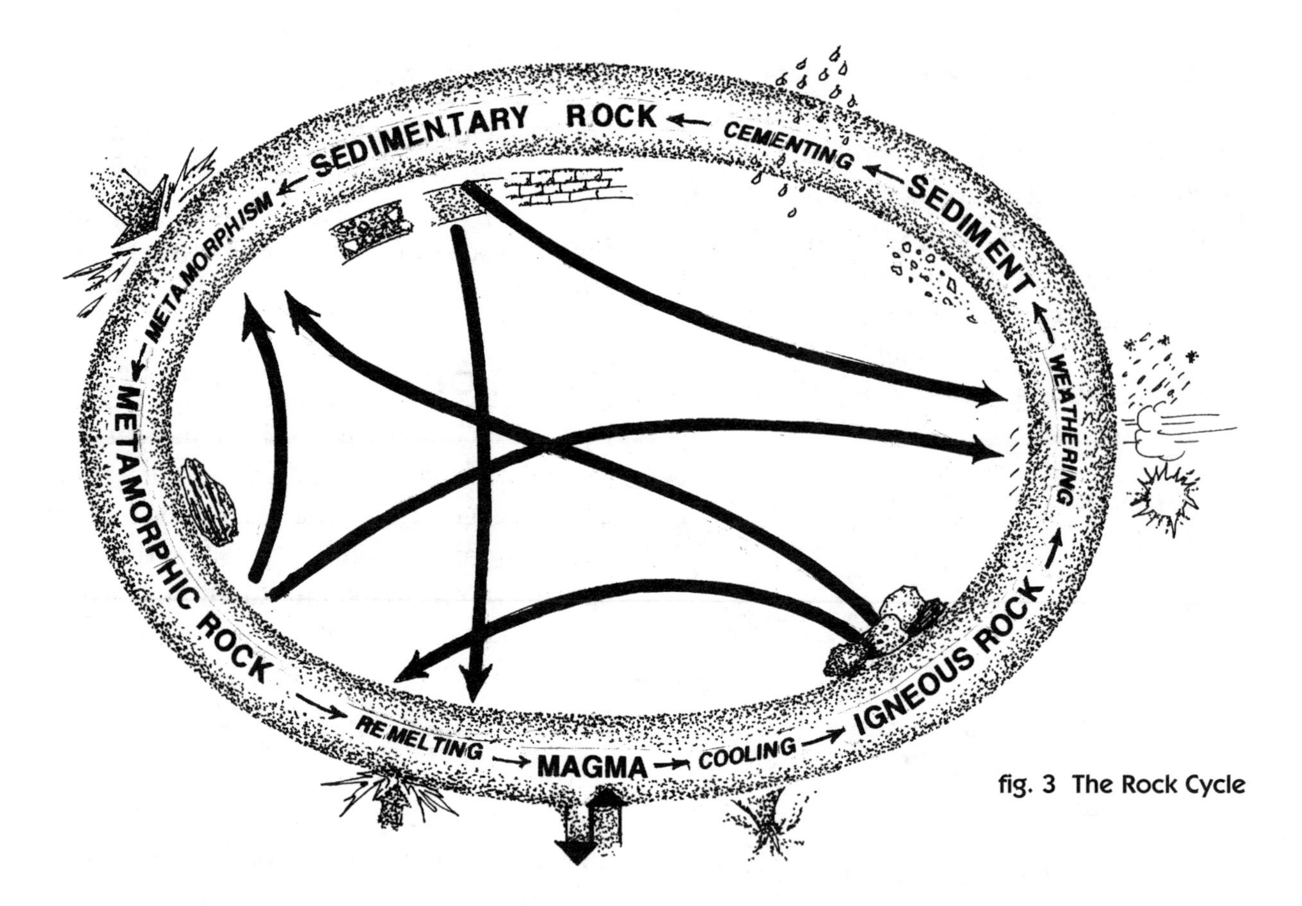

fig. 3 The Rock Cycle

Introduction:

All of the rocks on earth are constantly changing through a process called the **rock cycle***. In this cycle, any one of the three classes of rock can change into any other class. The elements and minerals in rocks redistribute from one rock type to another. Here is a diagram that shows all the changes that are possible in the rock cycle.*

> *(Allow students to view the diagram. You may want to give further comments about the various types of changes outlined in the diagram.)*

Lesson:

Let's imagine now that you are a rock going through some of the changes in the rock cycle. Please find a spot to stand where you are not touching a wall, furniture, or another person.

> *(Turn on music—optional.)*

Let's begin by imagining that we are an igneous rock. Find a rock shape to begin with. Will it be sharp and angular or curved and smooth? Now, imagine that the rain is pounding down on you, the wind is blowing at you and wearing you away. See if you can let your body get smaller and closer to the ground as if you are wearing down into tiny particles.

Now the particles are being carried along by moving water. Let's all move freely through the room. Try moving backward...sideways...in a curved pathway. Now let yourself deposit somewhere and settle to the ground. *(Students sink to a low level.)* Feel yourself being pressed

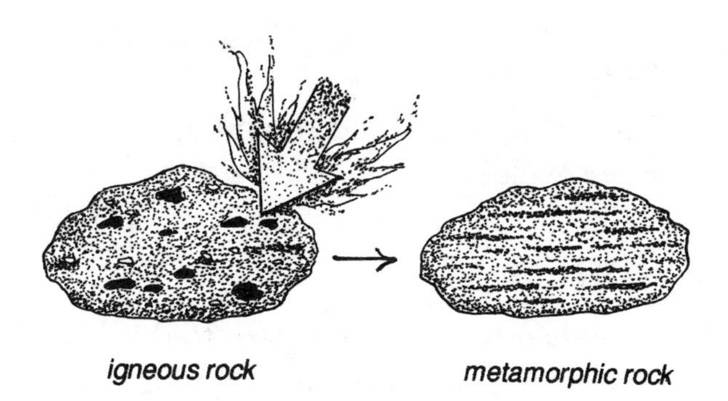

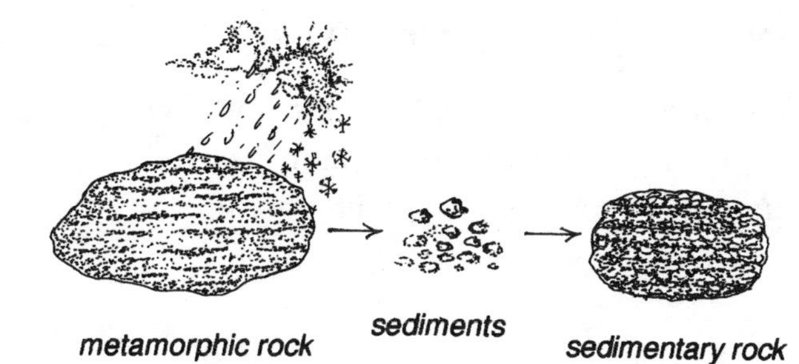

subduction
volcano
sedimentary rock
magma

fig. 4 Rock Cycle Segments

and compacted into a sedimentary rock. Feel how all your body parts are squeezing together.

Suddenly you begin to feel tremendous heat and pressure. Feel yourself being squeezed, bent and folded into a brand new rock shape. You are now a metamorphic rock.

Now heat from under the earth is melting your rock into liquid magma. Let your magma flow to a new place in the room. *(If you have limited space encourage students to make flowing, liquid movements with their bodies as they stand in one spot.)*

It's getting cooler and cooler, and the magma is starting to harden. It flows more and more slowly and...it stops. Now you are an igneous rock again.

(Turn music off—optional.)

You've just experienced one possible series of changes in the rock cycle. But, as you'll see if you look at this diagram, there are many possible changes that could happen. For example, an igneous rock could change, through weathering, erosion and deposition, into a sedimentary rock, which could then erode back into sediment. Or a metamorphic rock could erode and become a sedimentary rock.

In a moment I will divide you into small groups. Each group will get a card with one portion of the rock cycle on it. I'd like your group to show, through movement, the part of the cycle on your card. Your group will have to decide where to begin and end the cycle—perhaps you'll want to repeat it several times. You might decide to have everyone in the group be rocks, or have some people be the forces that are acting on the rocks. I'll give you about ten minutes to work on this. Be ready to show your work to the rest of the class.

(Divide the class into groups of 4-6. Give each group one of the 3x5 cards. Circulate among the groups as they work, giving assistance as needed. When all groups have finished creating their movement studies—approximately ten minutes—ask the groups to perform their studies for the class. Music is optional, but helpful.)

Conclusion:

After each group's performance, allow students to respond verbally to the following:

What part of the rock cycle do you think this group was showing?

How did this group show the forces acting upon the rocks?

How many times did the group repeat their cycle?

Variations:

You could add a spatial element to this lesson by having students move through the room in the spatial pattern of the rock cycle diagram. Then, in their choreography, they would also have to move in the floor pattern of their part of the cycle.

Extended Activities:

Ask students to create their own visual diagram of the rock cycle using a medium such as watercolor, pastels, or collage.

Section C: The Atmosphere

Our earth is surrounded by a layer of gases which we call the atmosphere. Earth's atmosphere is largely made up of nitrogen and oxygen, as well as some other elements in smaller quantities. Earth's atmosphere has long been believed to be the only planetary atmosphere able to support life as we know it.

Through a life-sustaining cycle known as the oxygen—carbon dioxide cycle both plants and animals are able to draw what they need from the lower layer of earth's atmosphere. Through airplane and space travel, however, humans have been able to journey into some of the outer layers of the atmosphere.

The gases in the atmosphere are constantly in motion. The atmosphere serves to circulate the sun's energy around the earth. The flow of the atmosphere's gases also creates winds, which affect weather and temperatures across the planet.

Though the weather can change on a seasonal or even daily basis, each portion of the earth is part of a specific climatic zone, which is based on its average temperature over a given period of time.

UNIT 1: STRUCTURE AND FUNCTION OF THE ATMOSPHERE

The earth's atmosphere is a cloud of gases which surrounds the planet. The atmosphere is divided into three major layers: the troposphere, the stratosphere and the ionosphere.

The troposphere, which extends six to ten miles above the earth, contains most of the atmosphere's oxygen and all of its life. The stratosphere is the cold, calm layer of the atmosphere where airplanes fly. Just above the stratosphere is the ozone layer, which filters out the sun's ultra-violet rays. The upper layer of the atmosphere is the ionosphere, which is comprised of the mesosphere and the thermosphere. This layer contains electrified atoms known as ions, and is where radio signals are bounced back to earth.

The major ingredients of the atmosphere are oxygen and carbon dioxide. These two elements, so vital for life on earth, are constantly being recirculated through a process known as the oxygen—carbon dioxide cycle.

The lessons in this unit provide experiences which describe the layers of the atmosphere, and help students understand the cycling of carbon dioxide and oxygen between plants and animals.

Lesson 10: Layers of the Atmosphere

Topic:
Troposphere, Stratosphere, Ionosphere

Type of Movement Activity:
Group Improvisational Exploration

Related Movement Concepts:
Weight (strong, light)
Energy (smooth, sharp)

Materials / Preparation:
CD player or tape deck

For this activity you will need to divide your movement space into three sections, each representing a layer of the atmosphere (see diagram on next page). This can be done using painter's masking tape, chalk lines drawn on the floor, rope or string stretched across the floor, or by dividing the space using objects such as traffic cones.

Musical Suggestions:
Troposphere: Flowing (see Discography)
Stratosphere: Light, airy (see Discography)
Ionosphere: Energetic, driving (see Discography).

Space Requirements:
This activity requires adequate space for the entire class to move freely, such as a gym, empty classroom, stage or outdoor space. This lesson does not lend itself well to adaptation for a smaller space.

Time Required:
Approximately 10 minutes

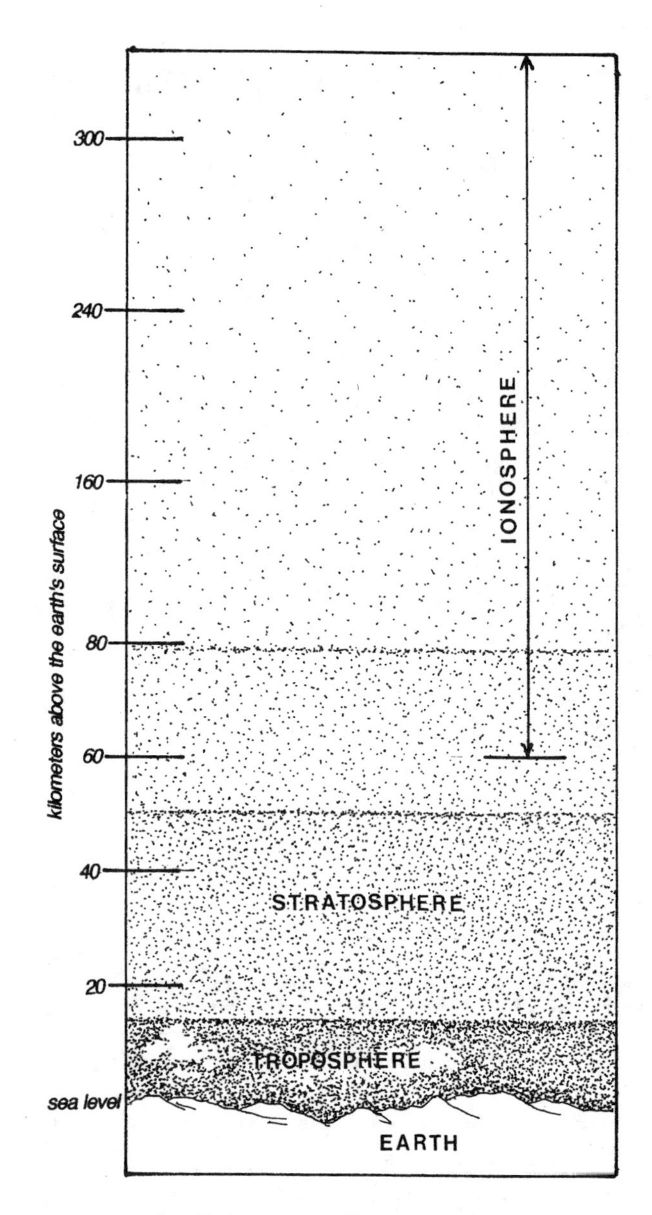

fig. 5 Layers of the Atmosphere

Introduction:

*Our earth is surrounded by a layer of gases called the **atmosphere**. The atmosphere is very important in making it possible for us to live on the earth. The air we breathe and the weather we experience are in the lower layer of the atmosphere, called the **troposphere**. The atmosphere has two other major layers: the **stratosphere** and the **ionosphere**.*

Lesson:

(Ask all students to find a place to stand in the first division of the space, representing the troposphere.)

The troposphere only extends four to ten miles above the earth, but it contains 90% of all the earth's oxygen. It is the place in our atmosphere where all life and all forms of weather exist, so there are lots of clouds and winds in this layer. It also has the densest air pressure of any of the three layers.

When I turn on the music, I'd like you to show me one of three things while staying in this layer of the atmosphere: You can either be a wind flowing and swirling through the troposphere, a cloud floating lightly or you can show me with your body how dense the air pressure is by doing strong pushing and pressing movements. After you've had a chance to move as one of those three elements of the troposphere, try the other two. Please continue until I turn off the music, then freeze.

(Turn on music. Allow students two to three minutes to explore movement in the troposphere. If necessary, give a signal for them to switch to a new type of movement. Turn music off. Ask students to step into the next layer, the stratosphere.)

The stratosphere is much colder than the troposphere, with very little oxygen. The air pressure is also much less dense, so all of your movements will be lighter.

At the lowest levels of the stratosphere, near the edge of the troposphere, there are icy winds blowing. I'm going to pick a few of you to be the winds. *(Choose four to six students.)* When the music begins you will flow and swirl like wind, but remember to stay close to the boundary between the troposphere and the stratosphere.

At the upper edge of the stratosphere is the **ozone layer**. The ozone layer filters out the sun's **ultraviolet** rays and prevents them from reaching the earth. I will choose several of you to be the ozone layer. *(Choose five to ten students.)* See if you can think of a way to form a filter or screen at the upper boundary of the stratosphere. Perhaps you'll use your bodies to create a line of connected shapes.

The rest of you will be in the main part of the stratosphere, where the air is very calm. You will need to move through the space very smoothly, slowly and lightly. Try floating, turning, melting and rolling. This part of the stratosphere is where airplanes fly, so let me have one person who will be an airplane. Will the airplane fly in straight or curved pathways?

When I turn on the music, please move as I've asked you to in your part of the stratosphere. When I turn the music off, please freeze.

> *(Turn music on. Allow students two to three minutes to explore their movements in the stratosphere. Turn music off. Ask students to move into the ionosphere section.)*

In the ionosphere, the outer layer of the atmosphere, the air is very thin. Your movement here will be lightest of all. See if your body can move so lightly that you hardly feel as if you're touching the floor.

The atoms in the ionosphere are electrified by streams of particles coming in through space, and are turned to **ions**. How could we show with our bodies that we are electrified atoms? Would your movements be smooth or sharp...slow or fast? Would you shake...poke...flick? Another thing that happens in the ionosphere is that radio signals are bounced to and from the earth. I'll choose two of you to be radio signals, and your job will be to travel carefully back and forth between the earth (one wall) and the upper edge of the ionosphere (the other wall).

When I turn on the music please move as electrified atoms in the thin air of the ionosphere, or as a radio signal if I've given you that job. When I turn the music off, please freeze.

> *(Turn on music. Allow students two to three minutes to explore movement in the ionosphere. Turn music off.)*

Conclusion:

Today we learned a little about the three layers of the earth's atmosphere. Which layer of the atmosphere did you find it most interesting to be a part of? Why?

Variations:

This activity could be designed by one class as a "walk through" experience for another class. To accomplish this, divide your class into thirds, with each third taking their place in one of the atmospheric layers. The second class would walk slowly through each layer, observing the movement in that layer. You might also want your students to create a taped "voice over" explaining what they are demonstrating in each layer.

Extended Activities:

Using what they know about the three layers of the atmosphere, ask students to write a short descriptive poem about one of the layers.

Lesson 11: The Oxygen-Carbon Dioxide Cycle

Topic:
The Oxygen-Carbon Dioxide Cycle

Type of Movement Activity:
Group Improvisational Exploration

Related Movement Concepts:
Place (self space, general space)
Shape (straight, curved, angular, twisted)

Materials / Preparation:
CD player or tape deck

Two pieces of colored construction paper stapled or glued together so that one side is blue, one is green (one set for every two students).

For this activity you may want to divide your space in half visually by using painter's masking tape, a chalk line on the floor, or a row of objects to create a boundary.

Musical Suggestions:
Music with two clearly alternating sections, i.e.:

Chapelle, Eric, "All and One" or "Tale of Two Villages," *Music for Creative Dance: Contrast and Continuum Volume I.* (See Discography)

Another alternative would be to use any selection from the Discography, turning off the music to signal the end of each group's "turn."

Space Requirements:
This activity would optimally be done in a large open space such as a gym, empty classroom, stage or outdoor space. However, it could also be done in the regular classroom with half of the students moving through the aisles and half standing behind their seats (see "Variations").

Time Required:
Approximately 10 minutes

Introduction:

Two important components of the earth's atmosphere are oxygen and carbon dioxide. As you probably know, all mammals, including humans, need to breathe oxygen in order to live. We inhale oxygen and exhale carbon dioxide.

Though carbon dioxide is a waste product to mammals, it is necessary for plants in order to live and grow. Plants take in our exhaled carbon dioxide. Their waste product is oxygen which, in turn, is vital to mammals. The constant circulation of these two components of the atmosphere is called the oxygen-carbon dioxide cycle.

Lesson:

I have some pieces of construction paper which have two colors: one side is blue and the other is green. *(Note: You may substitute any other two colors.)* The blue represents oxygen, which human beings and animals need in order to survive. The green represents carbon dioxide, which plants need in order to grow.

Even though we know that plants and animals live on the earth together, for this activity I'm going to divide the room into a "plant side" and an "animal side."

> *(Indicate to students which sides of the room are the designated "plant" and "animal" sides. Divide students into pairs. One of each pair will go to the animal side while the other stays on the plant side.)*

I'm going to give these pieces of construction paper to the "animals." When the music begins, they may dance on their side of the room any way they'd like, but they must keep the blue side of their paper showing to indicate that they are using oxygen. When the music changes, the animals will turn their paper over to show that they are exhaling carbon dioxide, then go to the "plant" side and give their paper to their partner. The plants will then dance in self space showing the green side of the paper. When the music changes, they will turn the paper to the blue side to show that they are exhaling oxygen, then give it to their animal partner. When you are not dancing you must return to your side of the room and remain in a still shape.

(Turn music on. Allow students to complete the activity as described above. It will be helpful to suggest ways of moving, i.e.: "Have you tried skipping?...hopping?...moving backward?" If you are using a single musical selection rather than an alternating selection, turn off the music when you wish one group to turn their cards over and give them to the second group, then turn the music back on when you wish the second group to begin dancing.)

Conclusion:

Today we did a movement activity that helped us understand the oxygen-carbon dioxide cycle. Who can now explain that cycle to us in words?

Variation:

This activity can be done in the regular classroom, provided there is space along the edges of the room and /or in the aisles between desks for students to move. In this variation, the half of the class who is not dancing will remain standing behind their desks. When the music changes or is turned off, the dancers will turn over their papers and set them on the desks of their stationary partners. Then the active group will go to their seats, and the roles will be reversed.

Extended Activities:

Assign groups of students to research other natural cycles, such as the water cycle, and describe them in words and movement.

UNIT 2: WEATHER AND CLIMATE

The atmosphere is the source of all weather and climatic conditions on earth. Weather is the constantly changing temperature, wind activity and moisture content of the air at any given point in time. Climate, on the other hand, remains stable over time, and is a reflection of the average weather conditions in a particular region.

Moisture in the atmosphere causes the formation of clouds and all forms of precipitation. Air masses move across the globe and collide, causing wind and weather changes. Atmospheric conditions are also affected by the sun's energy, an important component of the earth's weather.

The regions of the earth are divided into three major climates: Polar, Temperate and Tropical. Each of these climates has distinctive characteristics affected by elevation and proximity to large bodies of water.

In the lessons in this unit, students will be given experiences which will help them identify some major cloud types, understand air masses and fronts, and distinguish between several types of storms. They will also do research on the temperature, precipitation, and plant and animal life in particular climatic zones.

Lesson 12: Clouds

The choreography portion of this lesson is based on an idea by Anne Green Gilbert.

Topic:
Stratus, Cumulus and Cirrus and Cumulonimbus Clouds

Type of Movement Activity:
Group Shapes
Small Group Choreography

Related Movement Concepts:
Shapes (straight, curved, angular, twisted)
Relationships (near, far, over, under, around, through)
Weight (strong, light)
Levels (high, middle, low)

Materials / Preparation:
CD Player or tape deck
photographs or illustrations of stratus, cumulus, cirrus and cumulonimbus clouds (see page 38)
four sheets of paper, each with one of the following four poems written on it (next page)

Musical Suggestions:
Stratus: Constant, dense (see Discography)
Cumulus: Flowing (see Discography)
Cirrus: Light, airy (see Discography)
Cumulonimbus: Energetic, driving (see Discography)
Alternatively, choose one selection from Discography to use for all four cloud types.

Space Requirements:
The group shapes at the beginning of this lesson can be done in an open area at one end of a regular classroom. The small group choreography would optimally be done in a large, open space such as a gym, empty classroom, stage or outdoor space. However, it could also be accomplished by sending groups of students into separate areas of the classroom or into a hallway to work on their choreography, with the performance taking place at the front of the classroom.

Time Required:
Approximately 30 minutes

Cloud Poems

1. Stratus
   Flat, Layered
   Spreading, Stretching, Blanketing
   They turn the skies gray
   Stratus.
2. Cumulus
   Puffy, Soft
   Piling, Rising, Cushioning
   They are like a heap of cotton balls
   Cumulus.
3. Cirrus
   Feathery, High
   Wisping, Curling, Dispersing
   Sunlight shines through them
   Cirrus.
4. Cumulonimbus
   Heavy, Dark
   Gathering, Towering, Threatening
   Breaking into thunderstorms
   Cumulonimbus.

Introduction:

There are three major types of clouds: ***stratus****,* ***cumulus*** *and* ***cirrus****. Each type of cloud is different in important ways from the other two. One special kind of cumulus cloud called* ***cumulonimbus*** *is also known as a thundercloud.*

Lesson:

(Show photograph or illustration of a stratus cloud.)

Stratus clouds are flat, layered clouds that stretch like a blanket across the sky. These clouds usually form where a layer of warm air and a layer of cool air meet.

I will turn on some music, and ask several students to come up, one by one, and connect to each other to form a stratus cloud shape. When they are finished, we should see a shape that is flat and spread out. Try really stretching your arms and legs to create very straight shapes.

(Turn on "stratus" music. Call eight to twelve students, one by one, to the front of the room. As they come up they should connect to one another in a stratus cloud shape. When the shape has been completed, turn music off and ask students to take their seats.)

(Show photograph or illustration of a cumulus cloud.)

Cumulus clouds are puffy, like giant cotton balls. They form when warm, moist air is forced upward. Again, I'll be asking some of you to come up one by one to form a cumulus cloud. When you're done, we should see a soft, puffy shape that rises upward. Try connecting in shapes that are curved and rounded. Perhaps some people could be high and some low.

(Turn on music. Call eight to twelve students to the front of the room to create a cumulus cloud shape. Turn music off. Ask students to take their seats.)

Now take a look at this photograph of a cirrus cloud. It is very thin and wispy,

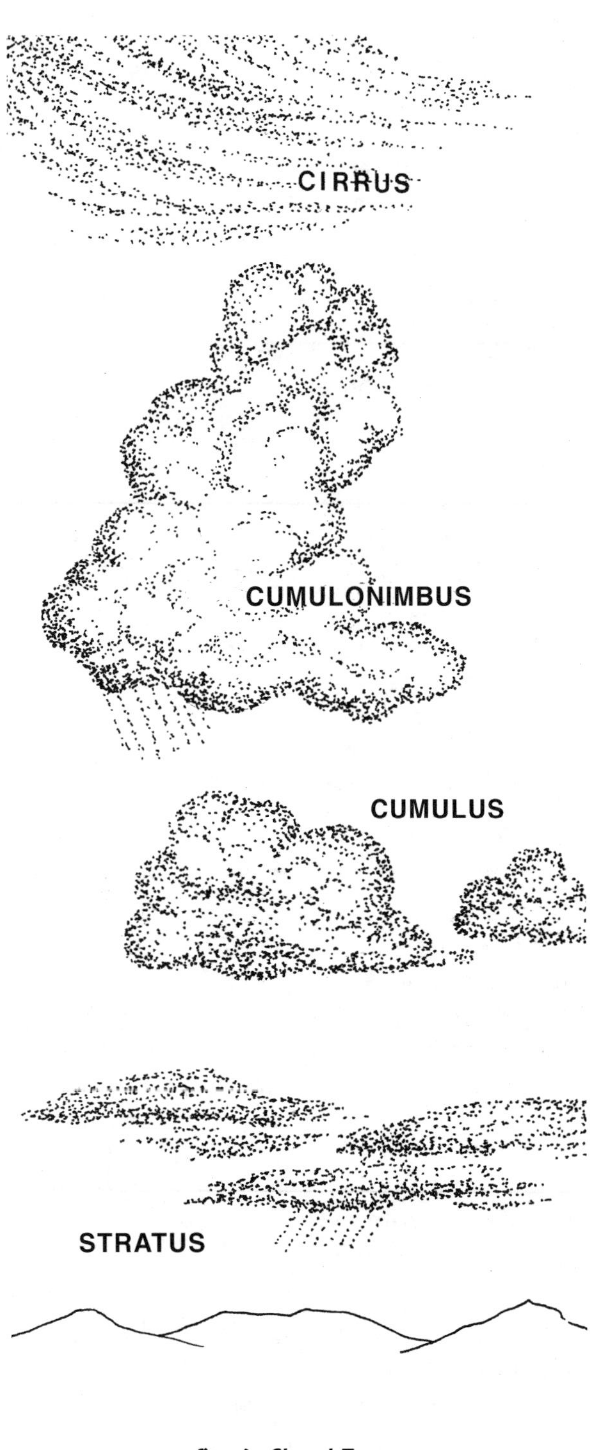

fig. 6 Cloud Types

almost like someone painted the sky with a feather. Cirrus clouds are very high, and are formed of ice crystals. The next people I call on will come up and form a wispy, high cirrus cloud together. See how light and relaxed your shapes can be.

> *(Turn on music. Call eight to twelve students to come to the front of the room to form a cirrus cloud. Turn music off. Ask students to take their seats.)*

The last type of cloud we'll look at today is a special kind of cumulus cloud called cumulonimbus. These are very tall, dark cumulus clouds that produce thunderstorms. They are often puffy on top and flat on the bottom. I'll have one last group come up to form a cumulonimbus cloud. Let's see if they can show us with their bodies how dark and heavy this type of cloud is. Try making shapes that are very strong and powerful.

> *(Turn on music. Call eight to twelve students to come to the front of the room to form a cumulonimbus cloud. Turn music off. Ask students to take their seats.)*

Now, instead of simply making the shape of each type of cloud, I'm going to divide you into small groups to choreograph movement to poems about these clouds. These are special five-line poems called cinquains. With your group read your cinquain carefully, then decide on a shape or movement to go with each word or phrase in the poem.

(NOTE: At this point, it will be extremely helpful to demonstrate this process by choreographing one cinquain with the entire class. For example:

Stratus *(all come together and make a flat stratus shape)*
Flat *(all melt to the ground)*
Layered *(all put arms over one another in "layers")*
Spreading *(all move away from each other)*
Stretching *(all stretch bodies wide)*
Blanketing *(all join hands in a line)*
Stratus *(all come together again in a stratus shape)*

In demonstrating the choreographic process, be sure to model collaboration by allowing several students to contribute their ideas, then negotiating which ideas to use and/or how to put several ideas together.)

(Divide students into four groups, giving each group one of the cinquains. Allow them ten to fifteen minutes to choreograph movement to their poems.)

Conclusion:

Allow each group to perform their poem to music. You could read the poem aloud as they perform, or they may want to speak their own poem. After each performance, allow the audience to respond to the following:

If you weren't able to hear the poem, would you still have known what type cloud the group was showing? Why or why not?

Were there any lines or words in the poem that this group showed in a surprising or unpredictable way?

Variations:

This lesson could be done as two separate lessons, with the group shapes taking place in the classroom one day, and the choreography taking place in an open space on the following day.

Extended Activities:

Ask students to observe the sky for a week and keep a record of the types of clouds they see. They might also write their own descriptive poems about their favorite type of cloud.

Lesson 13: Air Masses and Fronts

Topic:
Air masses and fronts

Type of Movement Activity:
Individual Improvisational Exploration
Group Improvisational Exploration

Related Movement Concepts:
Weight (strong, light)
Level (high, middle, low)
Relationship (near, far, over, under, around, through)

Materials / Preparation:
CD player or tape deck (optional)

Musical Suggestions:
Low pressure: Light, airy (see Discography)
High pressure: Constant, dense (see Discography)

Space Requirements:
This activity requires adequate space for the entire group to move freely, such as a gym, empty classroom, stage or outdoor area. To do the lesson in a regular classroom, have all students explore high and low pressure movements in self space (not traveling). The section of the lesson describing warm and cold fronts could be done as a demonstration by a smaller group at the front of the classroom.

Time Required:
Approximately 15 minutes

Introduction:

In our atmosphere are large, moving bodies of air called ***air masses****. Each air mass has about the same temperature and* ***humidity****, or amount of moisture, all the way through. Air masses can be cold or warm. The area where two different air masses meet is called a* ***front****. Different kinds of fronts cause different kinds of weather.*

Lesson:

(Ask students to find an empty spot in the room to stand where they are not too close to another person, a wall or a piece of furniture.)

Though you usually can't feel it, all air has weight and is pressing down upon the surface of the earth. Warm air is lighter than cold air, so it exerts less pressure on the earth. Please hold out one of your hands, palm up, to represent the surface of the earth. Your other hand will represent a warm air mass. See how lightly you can touch your "earth" hand with your "warm air mass" hand. This is an example of what air pressure is like in a low pressure area.

Cold air, on the other hand, puts more pressure on the earth's surface. Hold out one hand to represent the earth's surface again. Let your other hand be a cold air mass pressing down more strongly on the earth's surface. This is how cold air creates a high pressure area.

Now let's see if we can put the feeling of low air pressure into our whole bodies. Right where you are, imagine that you are very light; that your feet hardly put any pressure on the floor. Relax your muscles and feel like your arms are just floating in space. When I turn on the music, imagine that you are part of a warm air mass, and let that light, floating feeling carry you around the room. Warm air is so light that it rises, so see if you can show me movement that starts low and gradually rises off the ground. Can your arms move lightly...your legs...your head? Can you move both slowly and quickly when you are light?

(Turn on first musical selection. Allow students one to two minutes to explore the lightness of a warm air mass. Turn music off.)

Now let's try the opposite. Imagine that you are a cold air mass, exerting lots of pressure on the earth. Imagine that your feet are pressing into the floor, and that your whole body is pushing against the space around you. It helps if you really tighten or contract your muscles. When I turn on the music, imagine that you are part of a cold air mass and let that pushing, pressing feeling move you through the room. Try moving in different directions: forward...backward...sideways, or on different levels: high...middle...low.

(Turn on second musical selection. Allow students one to two minutes to explore the high pressure movement of a cold air mass. Turn music off.)

The area where two air masses meet is called a front. Different types of fronts produce different kinds of weather. First, let's explore what happens in a cold front, where a cold air mass pushes into a warm air mass.

(Form students into two groups of approximately equal size. Designate one group as the warm air mass, the other group as the cold air mass.)

Could I please have the people in the warm air mass crouch together on this side of the room. Cold air mass, please begin on the opposite end of the room. The warm air mass will stay right where it is and let the cold air mass come toward it.

COLD AIR MASS, you may begin to move very slowly toward the warm air mass. Remember that you are very dense and are exerting a lot of pressure on the earth, so stay fairly close to the ground.

WARM AIR MASS, when the cold air mass reaches you, you will rise up lightly to get out of its way. As the cold air begins to move between you, see if you can rise up on tiptoe and float slowly and carefully in the empty spaces around the cold air people. The cold air people need to stay close to the ground. Warm air, please be careful so that you don't accidentally step on anyone.

As the warm air rises it cools and produces clouds, so let's have the warm air people come together to form a cloud shape up high as the cold air moves underneath them. Cold air mass, please move all the way to the end of the room so you'll be out of the way.

The clouds in a cold front often produce heavy rain or snowfall, so could I please have the warm air people show me falling rain or snow with their bodies. What body parts can you use to show gently falling rain? Could you use your body to make the sound of raindrops? Perhaps you'll make the shape of a snowflake, and drift slowly to the ground.

You can see how a cold front produces clouds and precipitation. Cold fronts move through an area quickly, so the rain or snow doesn't usually last very long.

Now let's experience the opposite situation, where a warm air mass moves into a cold air mass. This is called a warm front.

COLD AIR MASS, crouch together right where you are. Be sure there are enough empty spaces between you for the warm air mass people to move through. You won't be moving at all this time, so make sure you're comfortable.

WARM AIR MASS, come to the opposite end of the room (where the cold mass began last time), and begin together close to the floor. Move lightly along the floor toward the cold air mass. Rise lightly and carefully tiptoe around the cold air mass people as they stay in one place. Once you are directly over them form into several cloud shapes. These clouds will produce very light, gentle precipitation. See if you can show the precipitation with your fingers.

> *(NOTE: The group portion of this lesson requires a great deal of trust and group cooperation. It is suggested that you try it at a time when your class is calm and focused, and perhaps has had previous experiences in moving cooperatively as a group. Also see Variations for alternative ways of presenting this lesson.)*

Conclusion:

Thank you, you may take your seats. Today we used movement to help us experience the difference in air pressure between a warm air mass and a cold air mass. We also discovered how air behaves in cold front and in a warm front, and why these fronts produce different kinds of weather. Who can tell us, in words, what happens when a cold air mass moves into a warm air mass? What happens when a warm air mass meets a cold air mass?

Variations:

An alternative way of presenting this lesson is to have the warm air mass people stand on benches or chairs which have been previously placed to avoid injuring students who are on the floor. For greater control it is also possible to do this lesson in partners, with one person acting as the cold air mass and the other acting as the warm air mass.

Extended Activities:

Ask students to create a series of drawings in comic strip style showing the approach of either a cold front or a warm front, and what happens when the two air masses meet.

Lesson 14: Storms

Topic:
Thunderstorms, Blizzards, Tornadoes, Hurricanes

Type of Movement Activity:
Small Group Choreography

Related Movement Concepts:
Level (high, middle, low)
Weight (strong, light)
Speed (slow, medium, fast)
Energy (smooth, sharp)

Materials / Preparation:
CD or tape player

Photos or illustrations of a thunderstorm, blizzard, tornado and hurricane (optional but helpful).

Four pieces of paper, each with information about one of the following storms:

Thunderstorm
- produced by rising warm, moist air
- cumulonimbus clouds
- heavy rain
- thunder and lightning

Blizzard
- freezing
- large amounts of snowfall
- strong winds
- deep snowdrifts

Tornado
- funnel of air extending from a cumulonimbus cloud
- fast winds traveling in a circle
- can lift cars off the ground, roofs off houses
- narrow funnel

Hurricane
- large, circular storm
- high wind speeds
- dense clouds and heavy rain
- "eye" of the hurricane (in center) is calm

Musical Suggestion:
Energetic, driving (see Discography)

Space Requirements:
This activity requires adequate space for all students to move freely, such as an empty classroom, gym, stage or outdoor space. Alternatively, assign groups their choreographic tasks in the regular classroom, then allow them a chance to work on their dances during an outdoor or gym period. The performances could take place at the front of the classroom.

Time Required:
Approximately 25 minutes

Introduction:

We are all familiar with the more common weather conditions such as rain, snow, wind and sun. Sometimes, however, unusual conditions in the atmosphere can result in more extreme weather including some very powerful storms called thunderstorms, blizzards, tornadoes and hurricanes.

We'll begin by learning a little about each of these powerful storms. Then we'll divide into groups and choreograph movement studies describing these storms.

Lesson:

One group today will be choreographing a movement study about a thunderstorm. Thunderstorms are caused when warm, moist air rises into tall cumulonimbus clouds, which look like high columns in the sky.

(Show a picture of a cumulonimbus cloud—see Lesson 12).

Because cumulonimbus clouds contain so much moisture they can produce a torrential downpour of heavy rain. The rain may be accompanied by lightning—a flash of light caused by electrical charges in the cloud, and thunder—a loud rumble caused by expansion of air when the lightning passes through the cloud.

I'd like the group who choreographs about a thunderstorm to be sure to show the cumulonimbus cloud forming, the heavy precipitation, the thunder and the lightning.

Our second group will be creating a study about a blizzard, which is similar to a thunderstorm but in freezing weather. A blizzard is characterized by heavy snowfall, driving winds and deep snowdrifts that can cover cars and parts of buildings.

(Show a picture of a blizzard or deep snow, if available.)

Perhaps this group will show some objects being covered by snow.

A third group will have the job of choreographing about a tornado. A tornado is a long, narrow funnel of air extending from the bottom of a cumulonimbus cloud.

(Show picture of a tornado, if available.)

The winds in a tornado are very fast and strong, and move in a circular path. The high wind speeds can cause cars to lift off the ground and roofs to blow off houses when the tornado passes over. Perhaps this group will show us some of the destruction a tornado can cause, as well as the swirling movement of the tornado itself.

The last group will be creating a movement study about a hurricane, which is similar to a tornado but much larger. A hurricane, like a tornado, is a circular storm with very high wind speeds. It is usually accompanied by dense clouds and heavy rain. The center of the hurricane, called its "eye" is relatively calm.

In a moment I'll be dividing our class into four groups and assigning each group one of these storms to create a movement study about. I will give each group a piece of paper that has some reminders of elements you might want to include in your study. I'd like each of your studies to have a beginning which shows how the storm starts, a middle which shows the most exciting and powerful part of the storm, and an ending which shows how the storm dies down.

Once I have divided you into groups, please spend a few minutes with your group discussing what the beginning, middle and end of your study will look like. Then begin to put your ideas into movement. Once you've finished creating your study, practice it two more times to make sure you will be able to remember it.

(Divide your class into four groups and give each group the sheet of paper with information about one of the storms. Allow approximately fifteen minutes for the students to create their movement studies. Circulate among the groups as they work, providing assistance as needed.)

Conclusion:

Allow each group an opportunity to perform. Music is optional, but very helpful. At the conclusion of each performance allow the audience to respond to the following questions:

Did this group clearly show what type of storm they were describing? What did they do to make that clear?

How did this movement study begin? Could you tell what caused the storm?

How did this study end?

How did this group show the climax of the storm?

What were some of the Movement Concepts this group used to show their storm?

Variations:

These studies could be further rehearsed and polished, and used as performance pieces to present to another class, or to perform in an all-school assembly.

Extended Activities:

Ask each group to paint a "backdrop" for their performance showing some of their storm's elements.

Lesson 15: Climate

Topic:
Tundra Climate

Type of Movement Activity:
Group Shapes
Group Improvisational Exploration

Related Movement Concepts:
Relationships (near, far, over, under, around, through)
Shapes (straight, curved, angular, twisted)
Levels (high, middle, low)
Energy (smooth, sharp)

Materials /Preparation
No materials or preparation required

Musical Suggestions:
No music required

Space Requirements:
This lesson would optimally take place in a large, open space so that all students could participate in creating the tundra environment. Alternatively, a smaller group could create the environment at the front of the classroom as a demonstration. You may also want to simply have your students do the suggested movements and shapes in self space, standing behind their desks.

Time Required:
Approximately 15 minutes

Introduction:

In contrast to ***weather****, which is constantly changing in any given location, the* ***climate*** *of an area consists of its more stable, long-term atmospheric patterns. The climate of an area is classified according to its temperature and the amount of moisture or* ***precipitation*** *in the atmosphere.*

Scientist have divided the climates of the earth in many different ways, but we can think of the earth as having three major climate zones, each based on the average temperatures in an area. These climates are the polar climate, which has very cold average temperatures, the temperate climate, which has moderate temperatures, and the tropical climate, which has the warmest temperatures.

Each of these three major climate zones are further divided into sub-climates according to the amount of moisture or precipitation in the atmosphere and the types of plant and animal life found in that area.

Lesson:

(Ask students to stand up behind their chairs.)

I'm going to tell you a little bit about the tundra climate, one of the sub-climates of the Polar climate. As I speak, I'll give you a chance to interpret some of the things I talk about in movement and shapes. Please do this right where you are, without traveling.

In the tundra climate it is extremely cold—below freezing for most of the year. How would you show this with your body? Now try showing it in a new way; one that might surprise me. Could your body make a shape that says "freezing"? Would your freezing shape have sharp angles, curves or straight lines?

The precipitation in a tundra climate is less than ten inches a year, almost all in the form of snow. How could you use your body to show snow falling? Now try that movement with a different body part. How slowly can you make your snow fall...how quickly?

The plants that grow on the tundra are mosses and small shrubs, which are close to the ground. See if you can make the shape of one of these shrubs with your body. Perhaps you could join with someone else and create a low shrub shape together.

One of the animals that lives on the tundra is the reindeer. Try making the shape of a reindeer with your body. How will you show its horns? Can you move like a reindeer without traveling?

Think about a person on the tundra. How might that person be dressed? What kind of activity might that person be doing?

(Possible responses include sledding, ice-fishing, shoveling snow.)

See if you can show me some movements that a person on the tundra might do.

Now we're going to create our own complete tundra scene. First I'd like to have a few people come up and represent the freezing temperatures of the tundra. You may do this as a shape or with a movement.

Now I need several people to represent the falling snow.

Next let's add some low shrubs.

Now we need to add a few reindeer moving through the tundra.

Would the rest of you please come up and be people who are on the tundra. Show in movement what the people are doing there.

> *(Now the scene is complete. Allow students to continue their shapes and movements for a minute or two.)*

Conclusion:

We just learned about some elements of the tundra climate. What are some differences between the tundra climate and the climate that we live in?

Variations:

You may choose to repeat this activity with several more climates. Some possible climates are: ice cap, subarctic, marine west coast, desert, steppe, mediterranean, prairie, tropical rainforest, savanna.

This lesson can also be extended into a three-day project. On the first day the idea of showing elements of a climate through movement is introduced and specific climates are assigned to small groups. On the second day the groups meet to research their climate and plan how they will create a movement environment. On the third day the groups finalize their movement environment and allow their classmates to walk through it.

Extended Activities:

If doing the lesson as the three-day project described above, groups could create simple costumes or scenery to enhance their environment. For example, the rainforest group might use green crepe paper streamers to represent creepers and vines hanging from the trees.

UNIT 3: THE SUN'S ENERGY

Energy from the sun plays a major role in life on earth. As a matter of fact, if the earth did not receive energy from the sun there would be no life on this planet. Temperatures, which would be hundreds of degrees below zero, would be much too cold to support life.

The earth is about 150 million kilometers from the sun, yet the sun's energy is strong enough to reach us. However, the earth receives only a small portion of the total energy that the sun sends out. Some of the sun's energy is reflected, absorbed and filtered by earth's atmosphere. Some of it is absorbed by the earth's surface, which in turn may reflect it back into space.

In the following lesson, students will gain experience and understanding of what can happen to energy from the sun when it reaches the earth's atmosphere.

Lesson 16: What Happens to Energy from the Sun?

Topic:
Reflection, Absorption and Filtering of Sun's Energy

Type of Movement Activity:
Group Improvisational Exploration

Related Movement Concepts:
Pathways (straight, curved, zig-zag)
Relationship (near, far, over, under, around, through)

Materials / Preparation:
CD or tape player

Musical Suggestions:
Any selection from Discography

Space Requirements:
This activity works best in a large, open space such as an empty classroom, gym, stage or outdoor area.

Time Required:
Approximately 10 minutes

Introduction:

We've all experienced energy from the sun. When you sit outside on a hot summer day you can feel the sun's energy on your skin. Without the sun nothing on this earth would be able to live—the planet would be too frozen to support life.

The sun, which is about 150 million kilometers away from the earth, sends out energy in all directions. This energy travels in invisible waves, similar to the waves in water. Not all of the energy directed at our planet by the sun reaches the earth's surface, however. In our lesson today we will discover some of the things that can happen to the sun's energy when it reaches our atmosphere.

Lesson:

(Divide students into two groups and ask one group to stand against one of the walls of the room. It would be preferable to do this activity across the longest dimension of the room if it is rectangular.)

We're going to imagine that this wall is the sun, and that those of you standing against it are waves of energy from the sun.

The sun's energy travels in invisible waves, similar to waves in the ocean. Show me how you would travel to the other end of the room by moving up and down slowly in a curved pathway like an ocean wave.

(Allow students to move like waves to the opposite wall, then ask them to come back to where they started.)

We're going to imagine that the opposite wall of the room is the earth's surface. The space between the two walls will represent the space between the sun and the earth. The half of the room nearest the "earth" wall will represent the earth's atmosphere.

(Ask the students in the second group to spread out in the room and make an interesting shape. Each person should make sure there is plenty of space around them.)

The rest of you are particles of dust and water in the earth's atmosphere.

Part of the sun's energy that enters our atmosphere bounces off dust and water particles and is reflected back into space. When the music begins, I'd like those of you who are the sun's energy to move slowly in waves across the room. When you come close to one of the dust or water particles, imagine that they have an invisible wall around them which you bounce against gently and get sent back to where you came from. Please make sure that you don't actually touch another person as you bounce.

(Turn on music. Allow "sun's energy" group to move in waves toward the dust and water particles, bounce, and be reflected back toward the "sun" wall. Turn music off.)

Now we will experience how some of the sun's energy, rather than being reflected back into space, is scattered into the atmosphere when it hits dust and water particles. Sun's energy group, when I turn on the music I'd like you to move slowly across the room in waves again. When you come to a dust or water particle bounce gently against the invisible wall around it and let that bounce spin you into the atmosphere. You can keep spinning in the earth's atmosphere until I turn the music off, then freeze.

(Allow students to complete the above task. Turn music off when all the sun's energy has been scattered into the atmosphere.)

Not all of the sun's energy is helpful to life on earth. Gamma rays and x-ray waves would kill people if they were not filtered out by the atmosphere. Dust particle group, please take a moment to decide how you will prevent some of the sun's energy from reaching the earth. Perhaps you'll create a barrier out of connected shapes.

(Allow dust particle group a moment to complete this task.)

When I turn on the music, the sun's energy will travel slowly toward the earth again. Show me how some of the energy will be filtered out by the earth's atmosphere.

(Turn on music. Allow students to complete this task. Turn off music.)

Let's show one more thing that can happen to the sun's energy. Some of it actually reaches the earth's surface and is absorbed. When I turn on the music the sun's energy will begin to travel across the room again. Maybe they'll find a new way to travel this time, perhaps in a different direction or on a new level. They won't be stopped, but will make it all the way to the opposite wall, which represents the earth's surface. They might come close to a dust or water particle as they pass, but it won't stop them from moving to the wall. When they get to the wall, let's see if each of them can find a way to show that they are being absorbed by the earth's surface. Can you let your whole body gently sink toward the wall?

(Turn on music. Allow students to complete this task. When all the sun's energy has been absorbed into the earth's surface, turn music off.)

You've just learned four things that can happen to the sun's energy when it enters the earth's atmosphere. In real life, all four of those things might happen at the same time! As I remind you of these four possibilities, decide which one you'd like to show us. The sun's energy can be reflected back into space when it bounces off a dust or water particle. It can be scattered into the atmosphere by dust and water particles. It can be filtered out of the atmosphere, or it can be absorbed by the earth's surface. When I turn on the music, each of you be ready to show us one of those four possibilities.

Dust and water particles, I need a few of you to join together to filter out any harmful energy from the sun.

If your choice is to be filtered out of the atmosphere, please move toward this group as you are crossing the room.

(Turn on music. Allow students two to three minutes to show their movement choice. Turn music off.)

Conclusion:

Today we learned about four things that can happen to the sun's energy when it reaches the earth's atmosphere. Who can tell me what the four things are?

Variations:

You may want to repeat this activity so that the groups have a chance to reverse roles. You may do this on the same day or on a subsequent day.

Extended Activities:

Ask students to write a short story about an energy wave from the sun, and the adventures it encounters as it travels toward the earth.

Section D: The Hydrosphere

The hydrosphere includes all of the water found on the earth and in the earth's atmosphere. Most of the water on earth is found in its oceans, but water can also be found in lakes, rivers and streams, in the form of ice and snow, under the ground as groundwater and in the atmosphere as water vapor. Of the earth's spheres the hydrosphere is unusual because it contains all three states of matter: solid (ice and snow), liquid (fresh and salt water) and gas (water vapor).

Water is continually being cycled from the earth's surface to the atmosphere and back through the processes of evaporation and precipitation. The combination of these two processes is known as the water cycle.

A relatively small percentage of the earth's liquid water is freshwater, and is found in many forms and locations both above and below the ground. Fresh water is found as groundwater and runoff, in springs, geysers, streams, lakes and rivers.

The largest percentage of the liquid water on the earth's surface is saltwater, and is found in oceans and seas. Beneath the surface of an ocean the land dips and rises in trenches and ridges. The depth of ocean water near the shore is affected by the gravitational pull of the sun and moon, which results in high and low tides.

UNIT 1: THE WATER CYCLE

Since the time the earth was formed, water has been cycling continuously between the earth's surface and the atmosphere. This cycling process, known as the water cycle, begins when heat from the sun causes water to evaporate from the oceans and other bodies of water on the earth's surface, as well as from soil and the leaves of plants. This evaporated water turns into an invisible vapor which later cools and condenses into clouds. As the clouds continue to cool, the vapor forms into water droplets or ice crystals and falls back to the earth in the form of rain or snow.

In this unit students will explore the cyclical nature of the earth's water supply through movement.

Lesson 17: The Water Cycle

This lesson was inspired by a dance activity created by Alina Rossano.

Topic:
Evaporation, Precipitation

Type of Movement Activity:
Group Improvisational Exploration

Related Movement Concepts:
Level (high, middle, low)
Weight (strong, light)
Relationships (near, far, over, under, around, through)

Materials / Preparation:
CD or tape player

Musical Suggestions:
Chappelle, Eric, "All and One," *Music for Creative Dance: Contrast and Continuum, Volume I* (see Discography).

Any selection from Discography

Space Requirements:
Though this lesson would most optimally take place in an open classroom, gym, stage or outdoor area, it can also be done successfully in the aisles of a regular classroom, with students performing the movements in place as opposed to traveling.

Time Required:
Approximately 10 minutes

Introduction:

The earth's water is constantly moving between the atmosphere and the oceans, lakes and rivers on the earth's surface. As the sun heats up the earth, liquid from these bodies of water, as well as water in the soil, ***evaporates*** *or changes from a liquid to an invisible gas called* ***vapor*** *in the atmosphere. As the vapor rises to where the air is cooler, it* ***condenses*** *and forms clouds. When the clouds get even cooler, the invisible water vapor turns into drops of rain or flakes of snow and falls back to earth. The constant movement of water between the earth and the atmosphere is known as the* ***water cycle****.*

Lesson:

(Direct students to find an empty place in the room where they are not too close to a wall, a piece of furniture or another person. If doing this activity in the regular classroom, ask students to push in their chairs and stand behind their desks or in the aisles.)

We're going to begin today by thinking about some places where water can be found on the earth's surface. Who can tell me one of those places?

(Possible answers include oceans, rivers, lakes, ponds, droplets on leaves, water in soil, etc.)

I'd like you to choose one of those places now as we begin our water cycle dance. Please make a shape on a low level. When I turn on the music, please move on a low level as an ocean, river, stream, or whatever body of water you've chosen.

(Turn on music. Allow students one to two minutes to explore moving on a low level as a body of water. In the regular classroom students may need to remain standing and do "watery" movements with their upper body if it is impractical for them to lie on the floor. If using the selection "All and One" by Eric Chappelle, go on to each succeeding part of the cycle when the musical sections change. If using another selection, allow the music to continue as you guide your students through the activity, moving on to the next part of the cycle when they seem ready.)

Great. I see people flowing like water on a low level. I see people curling, stretching and changing their shapes.

Now start to let your water evaporate. See how you can rise up to a high level and dance lightly, as if you are a droplet of water vapor. Let your fingers dance lightly…and your head.

Now, as you rise higher the air becomes cooler and you start to condense. See if you can begin moving more strongly, contracting your muscles as you push, pull and squeeze. Condense into a cloud that slowly keeps changing its shape.

The cloud is now so heavy that the vapor turns to water droplets, and it begins to rain. How would you show the raindrops with your body? Try making raindrops with your fingers...your toes...your elbows.

Now you're water on the earth's surface again. Think of a different body of water to be this time. Is it big or small? Does it move quickly or slowly?

Let your water evaporate one more time. Could you do it in a different way this time, perhaps more quickly or slowly than before?

As you condense this time, join with another person and create a cloud together.

Instead of rain, let's let snow fall gently from these clouds. How will you show a snowflake drifting slowly to the ground?

Let's end our water cycle dance by being snowdrifts on the earth's surface in winter.

Conclusion:

Now you've experienced the water cycle in movement. Who can tell us why it is called a "cycle"? What other cycles are found in nature?

Variations:

This activity could be done in a circular pattern in space to reinforce the concept of a cycle. The students would be bodies of water in one place in the room, the water vapor in another place, the clouds in another, with the precipitation moving them back to where they started.

Extended Activities:

Ask students to create a piece of visual art using the theme of "cycles." The medium for this artwork could be watercolor, pastels, chalk or crayon.

UNIT 2: FRESHWATER

Most of the earth's water is found in its oceans and is salty. A much smaller percentage is found on or under the earth's surface as freshwater. On the earth's surface freshwater can take many different forms. Some of it collects in still lakes, ponds and marshes. Some of it flows in brooks, streams and rivers. Some of it is frozen in icebergs and glaciers.

Not all freshwater is found on the surface of the earth. In fact, most of it soaks into the ground and into the tiny pore spaces in rocks and soil. It then becomes part of the groundwater supply. Water descends into the earth until it reaches impermeable rock, which will not allow it to pass through. It begins to collect above the impermeable rock until it saturates the soil. The upper boundary of this saturated soil is called the water table.

The water that is found on the earth's surface eventually makes its way back to the ocean by way of the earth's rivers. Each river has a life cycle which includes its youth—the time when it first carves out a channel in rock, its maturity—when it forms meanders, and its old age—when it widens into a floodplain.

In this unit, students will define freshwater vocabulary words through movement and explore the life cycle of a river.

Lesson 18: Freshwater Vocabulary

Topic:
Freshwater vocabulary

Type of Movement Activity:
Small Group Choreography

Related Movement Concepts:
Levels (high, middle, low)
Relationships (near, far, over, under, around, through)
Speed (slow, medium, fast)

Materials / Preparation:
CD or tape player

3x5 cards, one for every group of three or four students, each with one of the vocabulary definitions printed on it. (see page 55)

Musical Suggestions:
Flowing (see Discography)

Space Requirements:
This lesson would optimally take place in an empty classroom, gym, stage or outdoor area, but could also take place in the aisles of a regular classroom. In this situation, allow the groups to choreograph their dances in separate areas of the classroom or in a hallway, then have the groups perform their dances one at a time at the front of the classroom.

Time Required:
Approximately 25 minutes

Vocabulary Definitions

groundwater—precipitation that sinks into the ground and forms underground pools.

runoff—precipitation that flows off the surface of the earth and eventually reaches the ocean.

freshwater— water that contains no salt because salt is left behind when ocean water evaporates.

impermeable rock—rock that is too solid to let water pass through.

water table—upper boundary of the water that collects and completely soaks a layer of the earth's crust.

spring—a place where water flows out of the ground through an opening in the surface.

geyser—water and steam that build up pressure underground, then blast into the air through an opening in the earth's crust.

river—steadily moving body of freshwater that empties into the ocean.

tributaries—streams and smaller rivers that empty into larger rivers.

Write these vocabulary words, without their definitions, on the chalkboard or on butcher paper. *(NOTE: Feel free to add or delete specific vocabulary words according to the needs of your students.)*

Introduction:

In the study of the earth's freshwater, there are many new and interesting words to be learned such as groundwater, runoff, water table and tributary.

Lesson:

Today you'll have a chance to work with a small group to create a movement study defining one of the words on the board. Before I divide the class into groups, I'd like our whole class to create a movement definition together so you can see how it works. Let's create a movement study about a glacier using this definition:

> **glacier**—a slowly moving mass of ice and snow that gouges and wears down the land as it moves.

We'll certainly need some people to be the glacier in this study. Is there anything else that we might want to have another group represent? Yes, maybe we could have one group be the land that gets worn down as the glacier moves.

> *(Continue to work with your students' suggestions in creating a movement definition of the word "glacier" which they can all perform together. A possible scenario would be to have one group of students connect in a shape and move slowly across the room as a glacier. Another group could make shapes along the glacier's path, and show how those shapes are warn away when the glacier passes by. Be sure to use suggestions from the students, and to model creating a collaborative product.)*

You see how exciting it can be to show a simple definition if you do it with movement!

Now I will divide the class into groups of three or four and give each group a card with a freshwater vocabulary word and its definition on it. Each group will have the job of demonstrating their definition in movement. Be sure to decide what elements you need to include to make your definition clear. For example, if your word were "pond," would you just want to show the pond itself, or to include something in or near the pond as well? Also think about what Movement Concepts might help you make your definition clear. Do you need to travel at a particular Speed, or on a certain Level? *(NOTE: It is helpful to have a chart of the Movement Concepts on display for inspiration when you do this or any other movement activity.)*

(Divide the class into groups of three or four, giving each group a card with a vocabulary word and definition on it. Allow the groups approximately ten minutes to create their definitions. Circulate among the groups, providing assistance as needed.)

Conclusion:

Allow each group to perform their movement definition to music. After each group has completed their movement definition, ask the audience to respond to the following questions:

Which vocabulary word was this group showing? How do you know?

Who can tell me the definition of this group's vocabulary word? What part of the definition did the group show most clearly?

What Movement Concepts did this group use in their definition?

Variations:

This same activity could be repeated using vocabulary words from another area of the curriculum. For example, it could be used to review vocabulary from a social studies unit.

Extended Activities:

Ask students to write a paragraph about freshwater using at least four of the vocabulary words from this activity. Their paragraph should clearly demonstrate their understanding of those words.

Lesson 19: The Life of a River

Topic:
Youth, Maturity and Old Age of Rivers

Type of Movement Activity:
Group Improvisational Exploration

Related Movement Concepts:
Size (big, medium, little)
Pathways (straight, curved, zig-zag)
Relationships (near, far, over, under, around, through)
Weight (strong, light)

Materials / Preparation:
CD or tape player

Musical Suggestions:
Flowing (see Discography)

Space Requirements:
This lesson would optimally be done in an empty classroom, gym, stage or outdoor area. It could possibly be done in the aisles of a regular classroom if the movement pathway were carefully delineated in advance.

Time Required:
Approximately 5 minutes

Introduction:

All of the freshwater on the earth's surface eventually finds its way back to an ocean. In order to do this, it becomes part of a river. Every river has a life cycle. In the river's youth stage, it carves out a narrow V-shaped channel in solid rock. In its mature phase it develops ***meanders****, which are curves caused by the wearing away of the banks on either side of the river. In its old age the river has worn away much of its banks and covers a wide, flat area called a* ***floodplain****.*

Lesson:

(Direct students to line up behind you in single file.)

We're going to "follow the leader" as we go through the life cycle of a river. We'll begin as the river starts to carve a narrow channel through rock. When the music begins, follow me and copy my pathway and actions.

(Turn on music. Begin leading students slowly in single file, doing strong movements as if carving through rock.)

This is solid rock so you'll need to work hard to carve through it. What body parts will you use to carve out a path through the rock? Stay in a single line, because our river is still very narrow.

Now the river is maturing and beginning to widen, so let's stand two by two in our line. I'll continue being the leader. Now we are beginning to meander, so let's move through the room in a curved pathway. It's most fun if you lean from side to side as you move.

(Lead students in a curved pathway through the room. Try varying the speed and level of your movements, as well as trying different locomotor movements such as galloping or skipping.)

Now the river is entering old age, and is widening out over its banks. Please join with another pair, and begin following me four by four. Let's move very slowly as we spread out across the floodplain.

(Lead students through the room four by four. The preceding journey may have taken you back and forth across the room several times. Continue until you are approaching a wall.)

We're nearing the end of this river's life. Everyone spread out against this wall and make a shape to end our dance.

(Turn music off.)

Conclusion:

We've just had a short movement experience about the life of a river. Who would like to be the leader now as we try it again?

Variations:

When doing this activity in the regular classroom, map out a pathway that everyone will follow and decide on an area where each part of the life cycle will take place. It is helpful to verbally discuss this plan with your students before beginning the activity.

Extended Activities:

Lead a class discussion on how the youth, maturity and old age of a river might be similar to those life stages in humans. For example, you might begin by talking about how when people are young, they are trying to "carve out" their place in the world. Like the river, as people mature they move from one side to another, trying out many different ways of living. In old age some people tend to focus less on moving forward, and more on broadening their vision of life.

This is only one way of interpreting the life cycle of a river as a metaphor for human life. Be sure to allow your students to express their unique ideas. You will probably be surprised by the sophistication of their insights.

UNIT 3: THE OCEAN

Most of the earth's surface—nearly 71%—is covered by the salt water of oceans and seas. The major oceans and most seas of the world are connected, and actually form one huge body of salt water.

When looking at the ocean from above it is impossible to see what lies beneath the surface waves. But oceanographers have discovered that beneath the ocean lie the earth's deepest canyons, as well as its tallest mountains. The shape of the ocean's floor is known as ocean topography.

Deep below the surface of the ocean, temperatures become colder and water pressure increases. Light also decreases with ocean depth, so that the bottom layer of the ocean is in total darkness.

The surface of the ocean is characterized by constant movement. As well as the movement of waves, usually caused by storms, the ocean changes its level daily as the result of tides. These tides are caused by the gravitational pull of the moon on the waters of the earth.

In this unit students will create an ocean topography using drawing and body shapes. They will experience changes in water pressure related to the depth of the ocean and will explore the movement of tides as caused by the moon.

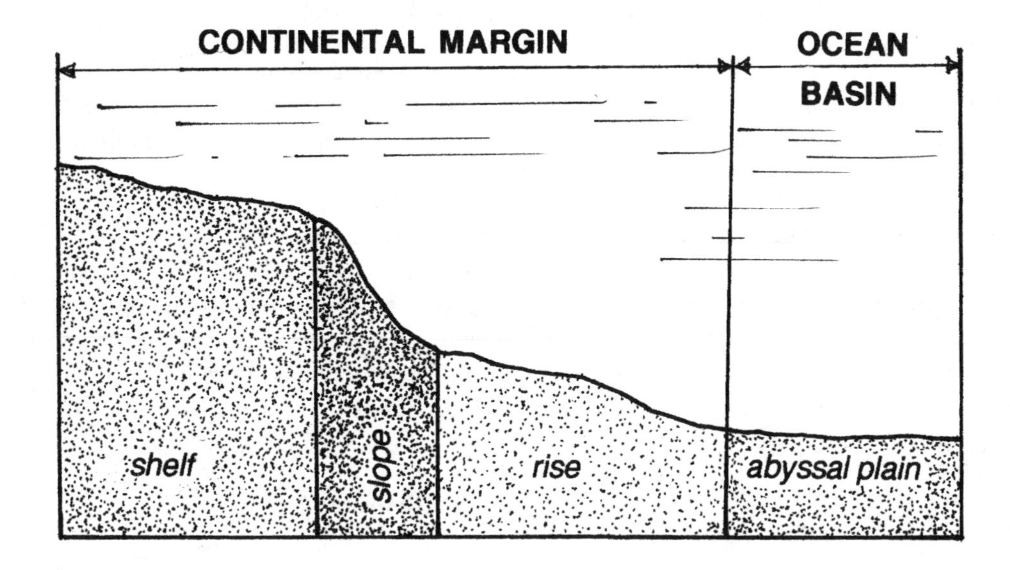

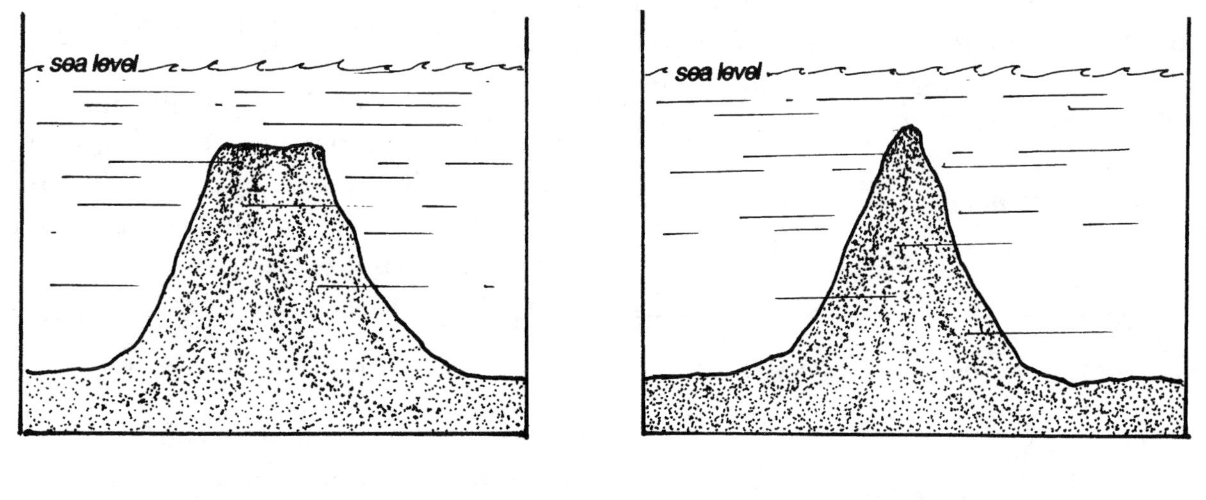

fig. 7 Underwater Landforms

Lesson 20: Ocean Topography

Topic:
Ocean Topography

Type of Movement Activity:
Group Shapes

Related Movement Concepts:
Shape (straight, curved, angular, twisted)
Level (high, middle, low)
Relationship (near, far, over, under, around, through)

Materials / Preparation:

CD or tape player (optional)

Drawings or diagrams of topographical features of the ocean floor (see opposite page)

Three large pieces of butcher paper

Markers or crayons

Musical Suggestions:
Ocean or underwater environmental sounds (optional—available on tape in many New Age or nature stores)

Space Requirements:
This activity would optimally take place in a large open space such as an empty classroom, gym, stage or outdoor area. In the regular classroom you may choose to omit the final portion of the lesson, which requires half of the group traveling in general space.

Time Required:
Approximately 15 minutes

Introduction:

Although we may not be able to see them, the bottom of the ocean is covered with landforms similar to those found on dry land such as canyons and mountain ranges. There are also forms that are unique to the ocean floor such as ***continental margins, guyots*** *and* ***seamounts.***

Lesson:

(Divide the class into groups of five or six students. Ask each group to find a place to stand where they are not too close to another group or to a wall.)

I'm going to be giving you information about five different landforms that can be found on the bottom of the ocean. After I tell you about each form, we'll try creating the shape of that form in our groups.

First we'll learn about continental margins. The continental margin is the area that separates a continent from the sea floor. The part of the margin nearest land is called the **continental shelf** because it is like a flat shelf of land reaching into the water.. As it slopes steeply toward the ocean floor it is known as the **continental slope**. Then it levels out at its base, which is called the **continental rise**.

(Show a drawing or diagram of a continental margin.)

See if you can work with your group to create the shape of a continental margin. Your shape should slope gently from high to low, then level out at the bottom.

(Allow groups a minute or two to create this shape. Call attention to the many creative variations in their solutions.)

Some of the tallest forms rising from the seafloor are called seamounts. These are underwater volcanic cones that sometimes reach all the way up to the ocean's surface to form islands.

(Show a drawing or diagram of a seamount.)

Try creating a seamount shape with your group. It should be very tall and cone-shaped.

(Allow groups a minute or two to create this shape. Comment on creative solutions.)

Sometimes the tops of seamounts have eroded down to sea level. When the ocean crust underneath them sinks, they are lowered well below the ocean's surface. These low, flat-topped underwater mountains are called guyots.

(Show a drawing or diagram of a guyot.)

Please work with your group now to make the shape of a guyot. Remember that it is lower than a seamount, and has a flat top.

(Allow groups a minute or two to create this shape.)

In several regions of the ocean there are trenches, which are like long, deep canyons. These **trenches** are often deeper than the Grand Canyon! They are usually surrounded by volcanoes.

(Show a drawing or diagram of an ocean trench, if available.)

How will you show an ocean trench with your group? It will probably help to show the volcanoes along the side of the trench.

(Allow students one to two minutes to create this shape.)

Did you know that there are huge mountain ranges underneath the ocean? The mid-ocean ridge system is the world's biggest and largest mountain range. Try creating a range of mountains with your group.

(Allow students one to two minutes to create a mountain range shape. Ask students to take their seats.)

Now we're going to work together to create an underwater landscape. Before we do it with our bodies I'm going to map it out on this piece of butcher paper.

(Tape or hang butcher paper on the wall so that it is clearly visible to all students.)

Let's start by deciding where our continental margin will be. It will need to be on one side of our seafloor landscape. Which side of the map shall we put it on?

(Allow students to suggest a placement for the continental margin. When a decision has been reached, draw a rough sketch of the continental margin on your map with a marker. Continue in this way, adding a seamount, guyot, trench and mountain range to your map.)

Now that we know where our landforms need to be, let's create this underwater landscape right in this room. Which group would like to be the continental margin?

(Choose one group to be the continental margin and guide them in positioning their continental margin

shape in accordance with the location on the map. Continue in this way with the four other underwater landforms.)

Now I will divide the class in half, and each half will have a chance to draw their own map and create their own underwater landscape in the room. Your group may not have enough people in it to show all five landforms, but try to include at least three.

(Divide the already formed groups into two large groups, giving each large group a piece of butcher paper and some markers or crayons.)

You have about ten minutes with your group to draw a map with at least three underwater landforms on it. When your map is finished, please decide which smaller group will represent each landform on your map, and how that group will show the landform.

(Allow students ten minutes to draw their maps and decide how they will show their landforms. Circulate among the groups, providing assistance as needed. When both of the groups are ready, ask one group to position their landform shapes in the room according to their map. The map may be hung on the wall behind them.)

Now I'm going to turn on a tape of underwater sounds, and the rest of us will be sea creatures exploring this landscape.

(Turn on music or sound effects. Allow the second group to "swim" around the landscape for one to two minutes. Repeat this process with the second group creating their landscape.)

Conclusion:

Today you learned about ocean topography. Who can name and describe one of the landforms found at the bottom of the ocean?

Variations:

The entire class could create an underwater landscape for another class to "swim" through. They might want to create a backdrop to go with their landscape.

Extended Activities:

Ask students to create a three dimensional ocean topography using paper mache or clay, which they can later paint.

Lesson 21: Water Pressure

Topic:
Water Pressure, Ocean Layers

Type of Movement Activity:
Group Improvisational Exploration

Related Movement Concepts:
Level (high, middle, low)
Weight (strong, light)

Materials / Preparation:
CD or tape player (optional)

Musical Suggestions:
Ocean or underwater environmental sounds (optional—available on tape in many New Age or nature stores.)

Space Requirements:
This activity can be done in the aisles of the regular classroom, as well as in a large, open space.

Time Required:
Approximately 10 minutes

Introduction:

Most everyone has had the experience of swimming near the surface of the ocean. It is very difficult, however, for humans and many sea creatures to swim near the bottom of the ocean for three reasons. One reason is that temperatures are lower the deeper into the ocean you go. Another reason is that water pressure increases with depth. Near the bottom of the ocean the pressure would be so great that it would crush the swimmer and make it impossible to inflate his or her lungs. A last reason that the bottom of the ocean is inhospitable is that it is in complete darkness because water absorbs light.

Lesson:

In our lesson today you will have a brief experience of how water pressure changes as you go deeper into the ocean. Since we can't actually "swim" in our classroom, I'd like to introduce you to the idea of moving on different Levels to help you imagine swimming through layers of the ocean. Let's begin by moving slowly around our classroom on a high level. This means our body is standing upright. We can walk, tiptoe, skip or gallop on a high level. We might even carefully do movements that take us off the floor, like jumping or leaping.

(Allow students to explore high level movement as you continue to speak.)

As you move on a high level, imagine you're swimming near the surface of the ocean. The water temperature is warm and there is not much water pressure so it is easy to move. There is plenty of light here. Please freeze.

Now we're going to begin moving on a middle level. When we're on a middle level we're halfway between high and low. We might be crouched over, we might be walking with both hands and feet on the floor or we might be walking like a crab.

(Allow students to explore middle level movement as you continue to speak.)

As you're moving on a middle level, imagine that you're swimming deeper into the ocean. The temperature is colder here. The water pressure has increased, so feel how you have to use your muscles to push against the resistance of the water. You might also imagine that it's darker here than it was at the surface. Freeze.

Now let's move on a low level, very close to the ground. You might be slithering on your stomach or back, rolling, crawling or scooting.

(Allow students to explore low level movement as you continue to speak.)

You are now at the bottom of the ocean. It is very cold and dark here. The water is pressing against you, making it difficult to move. You'll have to use all your strength to move through this water! Freeze.

In a moment I will turn on some underwater sounds so that we can really feel like we're in the ocean. When the sounds begin you can start to move carefully around the room on a high, middle or low level. You may change levels whenever you want to, imagining that you're going deeper into the water or swimming up toward the surface. As I watch you, I'm especially interested in seeing the water pressure change as you go deeper. I should really see you working very hard to move through the water at the bottom of the ocean. When the sounds stop, please freeze where you are.

(Turn on underwater sounds. Allow students to explore moving on different levels for two to three minutes. Turn tape off.)

Conclusion:

You just moved through the room on different levels, imagining that you were swimming in different layers of the ocean. Would someone please describe to me how it felt to swim at the very bottom of the ocean? How did it feel to swim from the bottom back toward the surface?

Variations:

This activity could be combined with Lesson 20 on Ocean Topography. Half of the class could create an underwater landscape for the other half to "swim" through. The "swimmers" would move on different levels, showing changes in water pressure.

Extended Activities:

Ask students to write a short story about a journey to the bottom of the ocean. The story would relate the adventures of a person or sea creature journeying from the ocean's surface to its floor.

Lesson 22: Tides

Topic:
Ocean Tides

Type of Movement Activity:
Group Improvisational Exploration

Related Movement Concepts:
Level (high, middle, low)
Relationship (near, far, over, under, around, through)
Size (big, medium, little)

Materials / Preparation:
Painter's masking tape, chalk, or a simple object such as a book to place on the floor to designate the "low tide line"

Musical Suggestions:
No music required

Space Requirements:
This activity can be done in an open area of the regular classroom as a demonstration using a small group of students. For the entire class to participate in the activity a large, open space would be necessary.

Time Required:
Approximately 5 minutes

Introduction:

If you've ever been to the beach you've probably noticed that at some times the water comes up farther onto the shore than at other times. This is the result of the ***tide****, which is what we call the rise and fall of the level of the ocean at a particular location during the course of a single day.*

This change in water level is due to the gravitational pull of the moon on the earth. When the moon is directly opposite a body of water on earth the water is drawn toward the moon, which causes the water level to rise and the water to extend farther onto the shore. This is called high tide. Once the moon passes that location the water level lowers until it reaches its lowest point at low tide.

In our lesson today you'll get a clearer understanding of how the gravitational pull of the moon affects the tidal level.

Lesson:

We're going to imagine that this open area is the coastline of an ocean. At low tide the water level comes to this point.

(Indicate an imaginary line on the floor about three feet from a wall. You may want to mark this low tide line using a piece of masking tape, a chalk line on the floor, or by placing an object such as a book on the floor. Ask approximately eight students to come to the open area and lie on the floor side by side, with their arms close to their sides. No one's body should extend beyond the low tide line. NOTE: Choose an appropriate number of students for the length of the space you're working in. They should be able to lie comfortably side by side from the low tide line to the opposite wall of the room.)

I'm going to choose one person to represent the moon. This person will start at the wall and walk slowly past the people lying on the floor, who represent the waters of the ocean. When the moon passes by you, I want you to imagine that a magnet is pulling you slowly to your feet. As you rise, let your body stretch out and take up more space. When the moon gets to the end of the line you should all be standing up and stretching wide. Then we'll measure and see where this ocean's high tide line would be.

(Allow students to complete this task. Once they are all standing up and stretching wide they should be stretching past the low tide line. Make another line on the floor to indicate the high tide line.)

Now the moon is moving away toward the opposite side of the earth. You may all slowly sink back to your original positions.

Conclusion:

Today you had an experience (or saw a demonstration) of how the moon affects the level of the ocean. Who can now explain to me, in words, the relationship between the moon and the tides?

Variations:

This activity could be done with the entire class representing the water and the teacher representing the moon. In this case, a large open space would be necessary.

The person representing the moon could hold a white balloon overhead.

Extended Activities:

Ask students to collect photographs of ocean beaches and coastlines. Create a class collage or display of coastlines with varying tidal levels.

Have students write a myth that explains the occurrence of the tides.

PART TWO

THE CHANGING FACE OF THE EARTH

The face of the earth is constantly being changed by forces from without and from within. The earth's rocks are constantly being broken down in a process called weathering. The smaller particles created by weathering are then subject to erosion, a process in which particles are carried away by running water, glaciers or wind. These particles may later be deposited to become part of a new land form

The theory of plate tectonics explains why the positions of the earth's land masses are slowly changing. Earth plates, which are like giant shell sections on the "cracked egg" of the earth, can drift apart, or they can collide to form mountains.

The force of a volcano originates in heat and pressure from the interior of the earth. Hot magma explodes to the surface and becomes lava, which cools and hardens to change the face of the land.

Section A: Weathering, Erosion and Deposition

The earth's surface is constantly being changed by the forces of weathering, erosion and deposition. Physical weathering, caused by temperature changes in the atmosphere, abrasion, and pressure from the roots of plants and trees, breaks down rock and reduces it to smaller fragments. Chemical weathering occurs when the actual composition of a material changes due to exposure to a foreign substance.

Erosion is the transportation of particles from one place to another by an agent such as running water, glaciers, wind or gravity. Most erosion involves not just one, but two or more of these agents.

Deposition is the eventual deposit of material in a new place by the agent of erosion. Deltas, sand dunes and moraines are examples of deposited land forms.

UNIT 1: WEATHERING

Weathering is the process by which the forces of the earth's atmosphere change the earth's surface. In physical weathering, the size and shape of rock is changed as a result of interaction with the physical environment, but its composition remains the same. In chemical weathering the composition of a material is changed through a chemical reaction, as when iron changes to rust.

In the lessons in this unit, students will experience through movement the differences between physical and chemical weathering, and will learn about some of the agents that cause physical weathering.

Lesson 23: Physical Weathering

Topic:
Physical Weathering Agents

Type of Movement Activity:
Small Group Improvisational Exploration

Related Movement Concepts:
Size (big, medium, little)
Relationship (near, far, over, under, around, through)
Weight (strong, light)

Materials / Preparation:
None

Musical Suggestions:
No music required

Space Requirements:
This activity can be done in one of two ways: If done as a demonstration for the class by small groups of students, the activity can take place at the front of the regular classroom. If all students participate in the activity a larger space such as an empty classroom, gym, stage or outdoor area would be preferable.

Time Required:
Approximately 10 minutes

Introduction:

*Though the rocks and mountains of the earth may look strong and indestructible, they are constantly being broken down through a process called **physical weathering**.*

Lesson:

(Divide students into groups of four or five, and ask each group to find an empty place to stand. If doing this lesson as a demonstration have four or five students come to the front of the room.)

One of the agents that can cause physical weathering is the temperature of the atmosphere. Warm temperatures cause rock to expand, or become larger. Cooler temperatures cause rock to contract, or get smaller. After expanding and contracting many times a rock may become weak and crack into smaller fragments.

Let's try showing this type of physical weathering in our groups. Connect in a shape with your group where you are all very close together. When I say "expand," slowly reach away from each other, staying connected. When I say "contract," shrink back together. When I say "crack," let your shape break apart.

(Say "expand" and "contract" three or four times, allowing students adequate time to reach apart and shrink together. After the third or fourth time say "crack.")

That's how the temperature of the atmosphere can break down rocks. Physical weathering can also be caused by the roots of plants or trees. Many rocks have cracks in them which are large enough for roots to grow between. As the roots get larger they press the cracks in the rock wider. Eventually the rock may break into smaller pieces.

Let's show that in movement. *(If doing this lesson as a demonstration, ask a new group of four or five students to come to the front of the classroom.)* Please choose one person from your group to be the roots of a plant or tree. The rest of you will make a connected shape, but be sure to leave a space for the root to fit inside. Now let the root squeeze into the crack.

Root, you are getting larger, so use your muscles to press the crack wider open... and wider...and now the rock breaks!

Let's learn about one more way that physical weathering can happen. This weathering process is called **abrasion**. Abrasion occurs when particles of rock scrape and hit against one another, breaking each other down.

In order to show abrasion your group will need to join with another group.

> *(If doing this lesson as a demonstration ask two groups of four or five students to come to the front of the classroom.)*

I'd like each original group of four or five to form a rock shape. There should now be two rock shapes standing side by side.

Very carefully allow your two rock shapes to come toward one another, touch each other's hands gently, and then move away. Try that again...and again...This last time make contact and then let both rocks break apart.

Conclusion:

Today you experienced (or saw) some examples of physical weathering. Who can tell me the three types of physical weathering you learned about today?

Variations:

This lesson could be done as a choreography project. The teacher would first explain these three types of physical weathering, then break the class into small groups. Each group could be assigned a type of physical weathering to show, or could choose one of the three scenarios to demonstrate in their own way.

This lesson could be immediately followed by Lesson 24 on Chemical Weathering.

Extended Activities:

Ask students to do "scientific illustrations" depicting how one of these forms of weathering breaks down rock. The drawings could be done using fine-tipped markers or colored pencils.

Lesson 24: Chemical Weathering

Topic:
Chemical Weathering

Type of Movement Activity:
Group Improvisational Exploration

Related Movement Concepts:
Place (self space, general space)
Shape (straight, curved, angular, twisted)
Relationships (near, far, over, under, around, through)

Materials / Preparation:
CD or tape player

Musical Suggestions:
Constant, dense (see Discography)

Space Requirements:
This activity requires adequate space for half of the class to move freely at a time. An empty classroom, gym, stage or outdoor area would be optimal. In a smaller space have students work in pairs. One student makes a shape while their partner moves around it, then changes and combines with it.

Time Required:
Approximately 10 minutes

Introduction:

In contrast to physical weathering where a material only changes its size, chemical weathering changes the composition of the material itself. A common example of physical weathering is rusting. In rusting, iron combines with oxygen in the atmosphere to form iron oxide, a totally new substance that is different from both the original iron and the oxygen that changed it.

Lesson:

(Divide the class in half, asking half of the students to come into the empty space and find a spot to stand. The remaining students should begin by standing against a wall.)

Would each of you in the open space please make a shape with your body. There are many types of shapes you could make: straight, curved, angular, twisted, wide, narrow...or your shape might be a combination of two or three of these types. The rest of you will act as chemical weathering agents that combine with and change these shapes. When the music begins, those of you against the wall will start to move around the shapes any way you want to. Try some movements that aren't just walking or running—maybe you'll skip, turn, float or shake around the shapes.

(You may want to demonstrate the next series of directions using one of the students who is in a shape.)

When you get tired of moving come up to one of the shapes. Only one person come to each shape, please. You are the agent that changes this material, so carefully move the person's body parts into new positions to change their shape. Gently move their arms...their head...their torso. When you have finished creating your new shape, find a way to combine with it.

You might connect to it, make your own shape over or under it, reach around it or put a body part through it. Hold your combined shape until everyone's combined shape is finished.

(Turn on music. Allow the students against the walls to complete the above task. You may want to suggest different ways of moving around the shapes and ways to change and combine with the shapes as the students move. When all pairs are in combined shapes, turn music off. NOTE: If there are an uneven number of students, two students could work together as an agent, changing and combining with the same shape.)

Look around and see how completely different these are from the original shapes you started with. Let's repeat this again so the other half of the class has a chance to be the chemical weathering agents.

(Repeat the above process with roles reversed.)

Conclusion:

Today you had a movement experience of how chemical weathering works. How is chemical weathering different from physical weathering?

Variations:

Instead of stopping the music each time, allow students to switch roles continuously: when a new shape has been created and combined with, the original shape disconnects and dances away.

Extended Activities:

Ask students to write a paragraph describing one of the following examples of chemical weathering:

rusting
limestone cave formation
chemical weathering of buildings in New York City

UNIT 2: EROSION

Once rock has been broken down by weathering, it may be transported to a new place by the process of erosion. There are several agents of erosion, including running water, wind, ice (glaciers) and gravity itself.

In the lessons in this unit, students will experience the process of erosion through movement and learn about some erosive agents and how they change the landscape.

Lesson 25: Weathering and Erosion

Topic:
Weathering and Erosion

Type of Movement Activity:
Group Improvisational Exploration

Related Movement Concepts:
Shapes (straight, curved, angular, twisted)
Place (self space, general space)
Size (big, medium, little)

Materials / Preparation:
CD or tape player

Musical Suggestions:
Flowing or Energetic, driving (see Discography)

Space Requirements:
This activity requires adequate space for the entire class to move freely. An empty classroom, gym, stage or outdoor area is recommended. The lesson could also take place in the regular classroom with students making shapes and moving carefully in the aisles.

Time Required:
Approximately 10 minutes

Introduction:

*The process of **erosion** plays an important role in changing the face of the earth. You may have heard of the land on a hillside being eroded by water. This means that water actually carried some of the rock and soil away.*

Erosion usually begins when rock is broken into smaller fragments by weathering. Once it has broken down it is more easily carried away by an agent such as water, ice, wind or gravity. This is how weathering and erosion work together to break down and transport rock.

Lesson:

(Divide the class in half, asking half of the students to find a place to stand with some space around them. The remaining half of the students will begin by standing against a wall.)

The people who are in the open space will represent rocks or rock formations. Would each of you please make an interesting rock shape right where you are. Your shape should be large, and on a high or medium level rather than down on the ground.

The rest of you will represent the temperature changes in the atmosphere that will weather and break down these rock formations. When I turn on the music you may move around the shapes any way you'd like to. Be sure to try some interesting ways of moving that aren't just walking or running. When you pass by a shape, carefully move one of that person's body parts a little bit so that the shape becomes smaller. Move a body part inward toward the center of the person's body, or gently move the person closer to the ground. Keep moving around to all the different shapes, making each one a little smaller as you pass. When I turn off the music please come back to a wall.

(Allow students one to two minutes to move around the shapes, changing them into smaller shapes. When most of the rock formations have been "broken down" turn the music off.)

Weathering has worked to break down these rock formations. Now the people against the wall will represent running water. When I turn on the music, move around the shapes once more. When you pass by a shape, tap it gently on the shoulder. Shapes, when you are tapped you will be free to move around the room with the water. When I turn the music off, everyone please freeze where they are.

(Turn on music. Allow students to complete the above task. When all the rocks have been tapped and are moving freely around the room with the water, turn the music off. Repeat the activity with reversed roles.)

Conclusion:

You did a movement activity today about weathering and erosion. Who can tell me how weathering and erosion work together?

Variations:

Instead of having individual students make separate rock formations, half of the class could make a large rock formation together. The remaining students would move around this large shape, pulling it apart into individual "fragments." The fragments would then be tapped on the shoulder and carried away by erosion.

This lesson could be combined with either Lessons 23 and 24 on weathering, or Lesson 26 on agents of erosion.

Extended Activities:

Ask students to write a short story from the point of view of a rock who is broken down by weathering and carried away by erosion.

Lesson 26: Agents of Erosion

Topic:
Water, Glaciers, Wind, Gravity

Type of Movement Activity:
Large Group Choreography

Related Movement Concepts:
Shapes (straight, curved, angular, twisted)
Place (self space, general space)
Flow (free, bound)
Speed (slow, medium, fast)

Materials / Preparation:
Tape or CD player (optional)

Four 3x5 cards, each with one of the following descriptions written on it:

a river carving a valley between two mountains

a glacier (large moving mass of ice and snow) carrying boulders down a mountainside

wind changing the shape of a sand dune

gravity pulling rocks down a cliff in a rockslide

Musical Suggestions:
Any selection from Discography (optional)

Space Requirements:
This activity requires adequate space for four large groups to choreograph simultaneously. The entire lesson could take place in a large open space, or each group could be assigned a separate space to work in (i.e.: a hallway). In this case each group could later perform their finished dance at the front of the regular classroom.

Time Required:
Approximately 25 minutes

Introduction:

The process of erosion causes change. Whether it's a valley being carved out of rock by a river or a ***glacier*** *moving huge boulders down the side of a mountain, erosion changes the face of the earth. The forces that erode the earth—water, ice, wind and gravity—are called agents of erosion.*

Lesson:

(Divide the class into four groups of equal size. Give each group one of the cards describing a change brought about by erosion.)

In the movement studies that you create with your group today, I'd like you to show how the landscape looked *before* the erosion, what caused the landscape to *change,* and how things looked *after* the erosion. This means that some people in your group will probably represent an agent such as water, a glacier (which is a large, moving mass of ice and snow), wind or gravity, while others represent the landscape that is being eroded.

Please work to make your studies interesting by using some of the Movement Concepts: What Speed will the movement in your study be? Will you be moving on different Levels or in different Directions? What Pathways will you follow?

(NOTE: Having a list of the Movement Concepts posted is extremely helpful when doing this or any movement activity.)

Because your groups are fairly large you will need to concentrate on cooperating and collaborating. Make sure everyone has a chance to state their ideas. Try to help the group move forward in making decisions rather than holding them back by disagreeing. Take a few minutes to plan your study in words, then get up on your feet and try your ideas in movement.

(Allow groups twelve to fifteen minutes to plan and practice their studies. If a group is still just talking after about five minutes encourage them to get up on their feet and try out their ideas. Circulate among the groups, providing assistance as needed.)

Conclusion:

Allow each group to perform their study with or without music. At the end of each performance ask the audience the following questions:

What type of erosion do you think this study was about? Why do you think so?

How did their landscape change from the beginning to the end of the study?

How did this group show the cause of the changes?

What Movement Concepts did this group use in creating their study?

Variations:

This activity could be done in smaller groups, with several groups being given the same description. It would then be interesting to see how each group solved the same problem in a different way.

Extended Activities:

Individuals or groups of students could work together to create three-part erosion pictures showing a landscape before, during, and after erosion. These pictures could lie side by side on a single piece of paper, or be backed on cardboard and folded like a screen.

UNIT 3: DEPOSITION

The final phase of the process that begins in the weathering of rock and continues with erosion is deposition, or the laying down of eroded material in a new place. Deposition is a major force in the creation of landforms such as deltas, sand dunes, moraines and taluses. The type of landform created depends upon the agent of deposition and the material that is deposited.

In this unit's lesson, students will learn about four types of landforms created by the process of deposition.

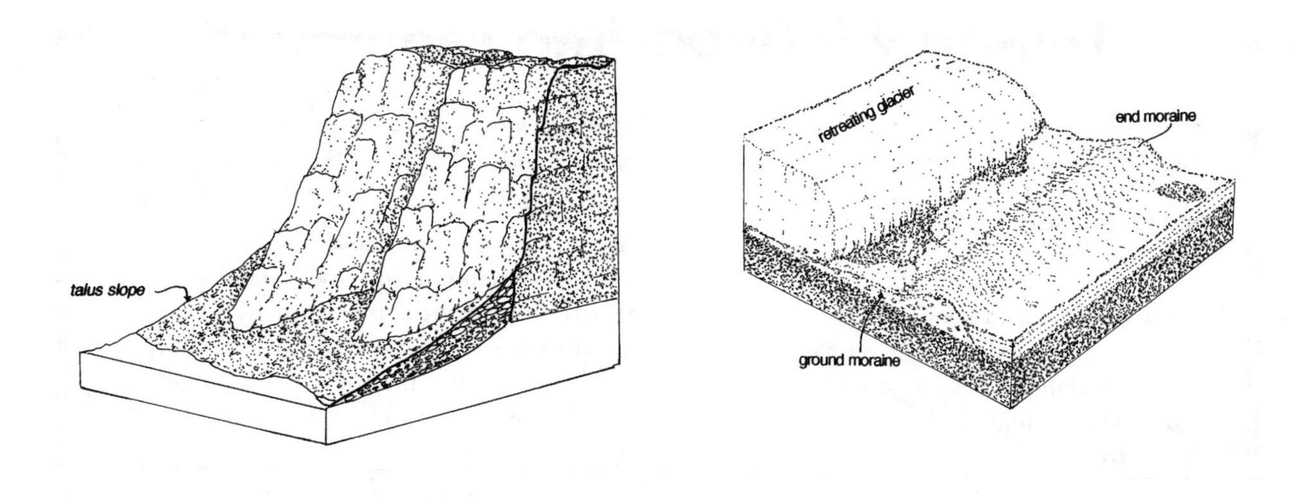

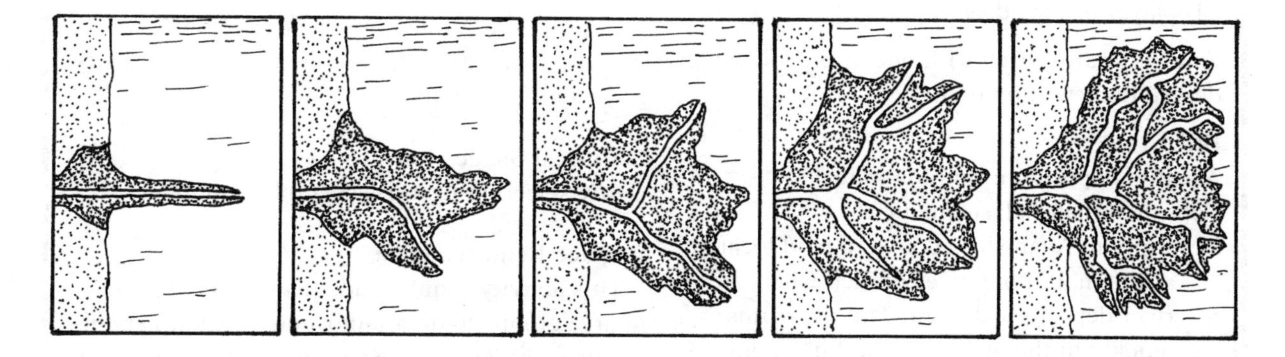

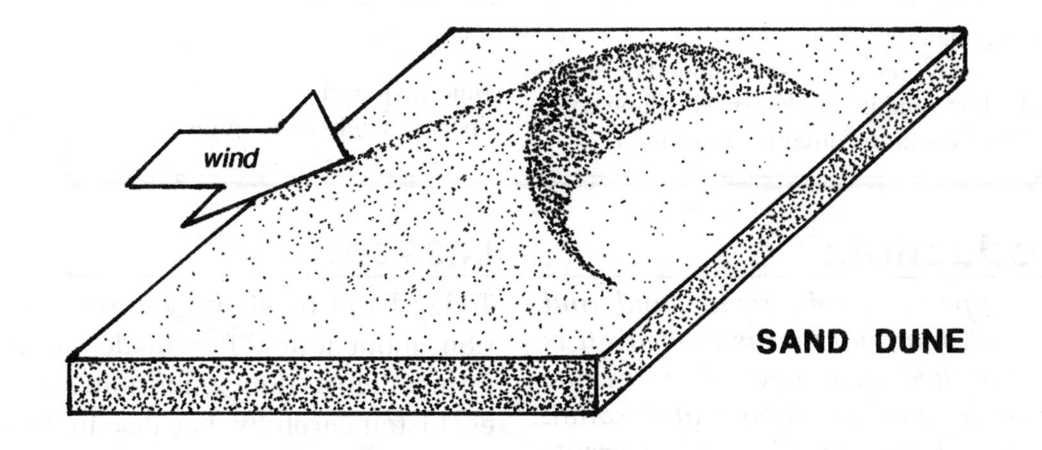

fig. 8 Deposited Landforms

Lesson 27: Deposited Landforms

Topic:
Delta, Dune, Moraine, Talus

Type of Movement Activity:
Large Group Choreography

Related Movement Concepts:
Shape (straight, curved, angular, twisted)
Pathway (straight, curved, zig-zag)
Speed (slow, medium, fast)
Weight (strong, light)

Materials /Preparation:
CD player or tape deck (optional)

Four 3x5 cards, each with one of the following descriptions written on it:

DELTA
Agent of deposition: running water
Deposited material: sediment
Description: A fan-shaped area of land located at the mouth of a river formed when the river deposits sediment. The river runs quickly in the mountains and hills, but slows down when it reaches the flat delta. It can no longer carry the sediment.

DUNE
Agent of deposition: wind
Deposited material: sand
Description: A crescent-shaped mound of sand deposited by wind in the desert. The dune continually moves in the direction the wind is blowing as the wind carries sand over the top of the dune and deposits it on the other side.

MORAINE
Agent of deposition: glacier
Deposited material: soil, rocks, boulders
Description: Material picked up by a glacier as it moves and deposited as it melts. The glacier pushes the rocks like a bulldozer or snowplow.

TALUS
Agent of deposition: gravity
Deposited material: rocks
Description: A pile of rocks formed at the bottom of a mountain, pulled down the mountain by gravity.

Musical Suggestions:
Any selection from Discography (optional)

Space Requirements:
This activity requires adequate space for four large groups to create movement studies simultaneously. The entire lesson could take place in a large, open space or each group could be assigned a separate place to work (i.e.: in a hallway). In this case each group could later perform their dance at the front of a regular classroom.

Time Required:
Approximately 25 minutes

Introduction:

What happens to soil, rock, sand and other earth material that is eroded? It is later deposited in a new place by the agent of erosion. Running water, wind, glaciers and gravity all work to create new landforms through the processes of erosion and ***deposition. Deltas, sand dunes, moraines*** *and* ***taluses*** *are all examples of landforms created as a result of deposition.*

Lesson:

Today I will be giving you some information about four different deposited landforms: deltas, dunes, moraines and taluses. Listen carefully, because in a few minutes you will be working with a group to create a movement study about the formation of one of these landforms.

I'll begin by telling you a little about deltas. A delta is a wide, fan-shaped area of land formed at the mouth of a river (where the river meets the sea). The river moves quickly in the mountains and hills, but slows down as it nears the sea and drops the sediment it is carrying. This sediment makes up the delta, which is an area of rich soil.

(Show photograph or illustration of a river delta—see page 77.)

The group who choreographs about the formation of a delta will need to show us the sediment being transported by running water. They will need to show that sediment being deposited in a fan shape on the ground. Perhaps they will also choose to show us the pathway the river follows as it travels toward the sea, and the changing speed of the river as it travels from the hills to flat land.

Another deposited landform which usually occurs in the desert is a sand dune. The sand dune is a crescent-shaped mound of sand formed by the wind. Once it is formed, the sand dune slowly drifts in the direction the wind is blowing. Wind carries sand over the top of the dune, then deposits it on the other side.

(Show a photograph or illustration of a sand dune—see page 77.)

The group who choreographs about the formation of a sand dune will want to show us the wind carrying and depositing the sand. They will want to show us the curved shape of the dune. They may also want to show us how the dune slowly moves in the direction the wind is blowing.

One of our groups will be creating a movement study about the formation of a moraine. A moraine contains earth particles of many sizes—pebbles, soil, rocks and even boulders. These particles are picked up as the glacier moves and pushed along as if the glacier were a bulldozer or snowplow. When the glacier melts, these materials are deposited along its edge in formations called moraines.

(Show a photograph or illustration of a moraine—see page 77.)

The group who choreographs about the formation of a moraine will show us how the glacier picks up and deposits material of many sizes. We should see the glacier moving slowly down the mountain, then melting.

Our last group will create a movement study about how a talus is formed. When gravity pulls rocks down a mountain, a talus or pile of rocks forms at the mountain's base. In this group's dance, we should see the force of gravity pulling rocks down the mountain and the pile that they form when they reach the bottom.

(Show a photograph or illustration of a talus—see page 77.)

(Divide the class into four large groups, giving each group one of the cards with information about a deposited land form.)

Your group's job is to use the information on the card to create a sequence of movement that shows the agent of deposition, the material being deposited and the form it is deposited in. Be sure that your sequence has a clear beginning, middle and end.

Be sure to give each member of the group a chance to contribute their ideas.

(Give the groups about fifteen minutes to create their movement sequences. Circulate among the groups, providing assistance as needed.)

Conclusion:

Allow each group to perform their study with or without music. At the end of each performance allow the audience to respond to the following questions:

Which deposited land form do you think this group was describing? Why do you think so?

How did this group show the material being deposited? What shapes and sizes were the pieces of material?

How did this group show the agent of deposition?

What Movement Concepts did this group use to make their movement description clear?

Variations:

This lesson could be done as a group improvisational exploration, with the teacher assigning roles and guiding the whole class through the formation of each of the four landforms in movement.

Extended Activities:

Groups of students could work together to create music or sound effects for their deposition studies. They could make tape recordings of themselves playing instruments or making vocal and body sounds (i.e.: clapping, snapping fingers, etc.). These recordings could then be played back as they are performing their dances.

Section B: Plate Tectonics

According to the theory of plate tectonics, the lithosphere consists of several rigid plates. These "earth plates" are slowly moving across the surface of the planet. These plates may spread apart, meet and collide or slide past each other, creating changes on the face of the earth. The end results of these movements are seafloor spreading—the addition of new material from deep below the crust when plates separate, the building of mountain ranges, and earthquakes.

The building of the earth's mountain ranges is the result of several causes. Some mountains originate when earth plates collide and fold. Other mountains are the result of movement along an earth fault, or crack in the earth's surface. A third type of mountain is built of layers of hardened lava.

UNIT 1: EARTH PLATES

The theory of plate tectonics, described in 1965 by J. Tuzo Wilson, states that the earth's surface is composed of several rigid, slowly moving plates each containing sections of the lithosphere and part of the mantle. As a result of this movement, one of three things can happen: 1. The plates may diverge, or spread at a plate boundary if new material is added from below, pushing the plates apart. 2. The plates may converge, or collide. When two earth plates collide one plate subducts, moving downward under the other, pushing up mountains and forming deep trenches. 3. The plates may transform, or slide past each other. Sometimes, when jagged edges of plates interlock, this sliding movement can cause an earthquake.

In this unit, students will explore through movement what can occur as a result of the movement of earth plates.

Lesson 28: Earth Plate Movement

Topic:
Divergence, Convergence, Transform Movement

Type of Movement Activity:
Partner Improvisational Exploration
Partner Choreography

Related Movement Concepts:
Relationships (near, far, over, under, around, through)
Level (high, middle, low)
Energy (smooth, sharp)

Materials / Preparation:
Tape or CD Player

Musical Suggestions:
Constant, dense (see Discography)

Space Requirements:
This activity does not require movement through general space and could be done in the aisles of a regular classroom.

Time Required:
Approximately 15 minutes

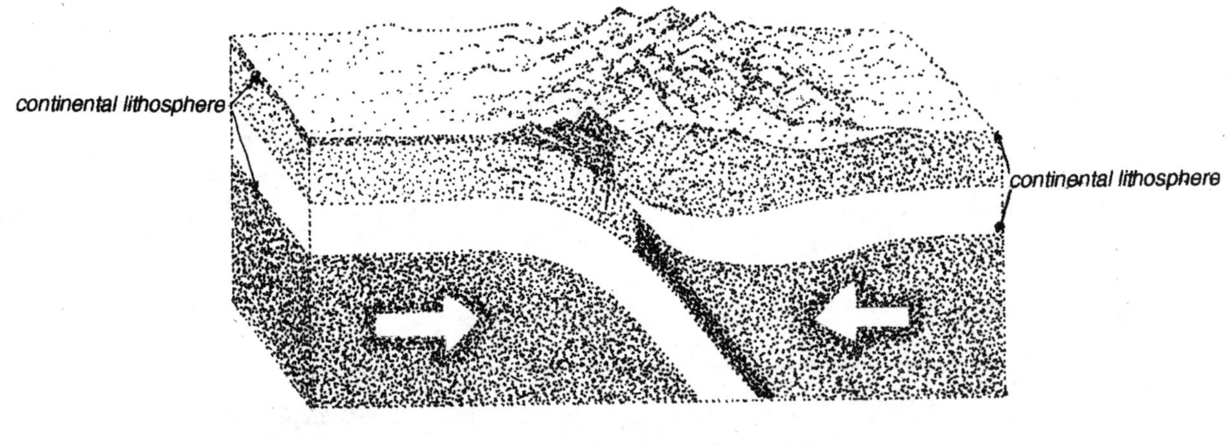

fig. 9 Convergence of Two Continental Plates

Introduction:

The surface of the earth is divided into large pieces similar to the pieces of a jigsaw puzzle. However, unlike a jigsaw puzzle, the pieces do move about. These pieces are often called "plates." Ideas about how these plates move, and interact with one another are called the theory of ***plate tectonics****. According to this theory, as earth plates move one of three possible things can happen: the plates might* ***diverge*** *or spread apart and leave gaps which then fill with lava. They might* ***converge****, or come together. When this happens, one plate* ***subducts****, or goes beneath the other, pushing up mountains and forming deep trenches. They might* ***transform****, or move past each other.*

Lesson:

(Divide students into pairs, and ask each pair to find a place to stand where they have room to take a few steps away from one another. Some pairs could stand in the front of the room, some at the back, some in the center aisle and others between rows of desks.)

Let's imagine that each of you is an earth plate, and that you and your partner are two earth plates that have come in contact with one another. Show me a shape where you and your partner are connected in some way.

(Allow pairs of students a moment to make connected shapes. This activity works best if students are standing, imagining that the air from floor to ceiling is the surface of the earth, rather than lying on the floor as earth plates actually would.)

Let's see what it's like when these two earth plates spread apart. When I turn on the music you will very slowly and smoothly stretch away from each other. As you are stretching, imagine that the empty space between you is filling with hot **magma**, molten material from underneath the earth's crust. When I turn the music off, please freeze.

(Turn on music. Allow students approximately ten seconds to slowly stretch away from each other. Turn music off.)

When two earth plates converge or come together, subduction occurs. This means that one plate moves underneath the other. Please take a few steps away from each other. When the music begins show how the two earth plates meet, then how one moves under the other. Since you are standing up, this mean that one of you will move behind the other. Show me how you think a mountain range would be created when the earth plates converge. How high will your mountains be? What body parts will you use to show them? Freeze when the music stops.

(Turn on music. Allow approximately ten seconds for students to converge their earth plates. Turn music off. There will be many different ways of showing mountain ranges. Because of their physical orientation, it makes most sense for the mountains to be protruding forward rather than "up." Notice and acknowledge those solutions that are particularly interesting or creative.)

Last of all let's show how the meeting of two earth plates can cause an earthquake. Sometimes instead of colliding and subducting the two earth plates transform, or move past each other, rubbing edges as they go. When this happens the edges may stick together, causing an earthquake.

Please take a few steps away from each other again. When the music begins, show how your two plates meet and begin to move past each other. Then show how the edges of the plates stick together and cause an earthquake. You might make your earthquake very dramatic, with lots of sharp trembling, shaking and collapsing.

(Allow students approximately ten seconds to show their "earthquake." Comment on interesting variations that you see.)

Now I will give you and your partner a chance to combine these three earth plate movements into a choreographed sequence. First you will talk with your partner and plan the order in which you'd like to perform your three movements. Then plan and practice how you will make a smooth transition from one movement to the next. At the end of your "earth plate" sequence hold your shape for a moment so we'll know you're finished.

(Allow students three to four minutes to plan and practice their sequences. Circulate among the pairs providing assistance as needed.)

Conclusion:

Allow half of the pairs to perform their sequences simultaneously, with music. At the end of their performance ask the audience members the following questions.:

Did any of the pairs choose the same order for their earth plate movements, or did each pair choose a different order?

Which of the four earth plate movements was your eye usually most drawn to? Why do you think that was?

Were there any surprising moments in the way the sequences fit together?

Were there any moments when all the groups were doing the same thing at the same time?

Reverse roles so that all pairs of students have an opportunity to perform their sequences.

Variations:

This activity could be done in larger groups, with several students joining together to create one earth plate.

Extended Activities:

Students could create three-dimensional representations of one or more of the earth plate movements using clay, paper mache or another pliable substance.

UNIT 2: MOUNTAIN-BUILDING

The face of the earth is studded with spectacular mountains and mountain ranges: the Himalayas, the Appalachians, the Andes and many more. All of these majestic landforms were created through one of three processes: folding—when rocks are bent due to subduction and high pressure, faulting—when rocks transform or slip upwards and downwards along a crack, and layering—when layers of hardening lava accumulate.

In the lesson in this unit, students will experience the three ways that mountains are built.

Lesson 29: Mountain-building

Topic:
Folding, Faulting, Layering

Type of Movement Activity:
Partner Improvisational Exploration

Related Movement Concepts:
Relationships (near, far, over, under, around, through)
Levels (high, middle, low)

Materials / Preparation:
None

Musical Suggestions:
1. A selection that contains alternating sections such as:
Chappelle, Eric, "Tale of Two Villages," *Music for Creative Dance: Contrast and Continuum Volume I* (see Discography)

2. Flowing or Energetic, driving (see Discography)

Space Requirements:
This lesson would optimally take place in a large, open space such as an empty classroom, gym, stage or outdoor area. For use in the regular classroom you may choose to omit the second part of the lesson which requires students to travel through space and simply have pairs of students show the processes of mountain building through creating stationary shapes.

Time Required:
Approximately 10 minutes

Introduction:

There are three basic ways that mountains are formed on the face of the earth:

Some mountains are formed through the process of ***folding****. When earth plates converge or when rock is under great pressure the earth's crust will fold. The upward part of a fold which forms a mountain is called the* ***anticline****, while the downward part of the fold which forms a valley is called the* ***syncline****.*

Other mountains are formed because of transform movement along a ***fault.*** *A fault is a fracture along which rocks may move. If the movement along a fault is up and down, one piece of the earth's crust will end up being higher than its surroundings.*

A last type of mountain is formed because of layers of lava hardening after a volcanic eruption. The layers pile on top of one another until enough hard lava has accumulated to form a mountain.

Lesson:

(Divide students into pairs. If there are an uneven number of students, ask one to demonstrate with you. Ask pairs to find an empty spot to stand.)

Let's begin by trying the first type of mountain-building, which is called folding.

Take a moment, without talking, to work with your partner to discover a way to show that you are two earth plates under such great pressure that you fold and form a mountain or mountain range. Carefully show how one plate subducts beneath the other, pressing the earth into folds. Since you are standing up, one plate will move behind the other.

(Allow students approximately one minute to find a solution to this problem. Indicate one side of the room, and allow the pairs on that side to perform their folding movement while the pairs on the other side of the room watch. Then reverse roles so that all pairs have a chance to perform their movement. The purpose here is to expand each student's range of ideas for possible solutions to the problem.)

Let's move on to the next mountain-building process, which is faulting. In demonstrating this process you will each represent an earth plate, with a crack or fault between the two of you. One earth plate will move upward along the fault, the other will move downward. Please take a minute with your partner to figure out how you might demonstrate faulting.

(Allow pairs approximately one minute to find a way to demonstrate faulting. Again, allow each half of the class a chance to observe the solutions created by the other half.)

Last of all, let's demonstrate the process of layering. There are several ways you could show this process with your partner. Perhaps you'll show a volcano erupting and the lava flowing and hardening to form a mountain. Or you could simply have one person harden into a shape with the other person hardening into a shape above it. Please do this without touching one another, or touching very gently. Take a minute with your partner to explore a possible way to show layering.

(Allow pairs approximately one minute to find a solution. Repeat the process of allowing each half of the class to observe the solutions created by the other half. Ask students to separate from their partners and find their own places in the room to begin the next segment of the lesson.)

You've just seen many possible ways to demonstrate folding, faulting and layering. Now you'll have a chance to try several solutions with different partners.

I'm going to play some music and give you a chance to move around the room any way you'd like to. Please try a variety of movements rather than just walking or running. When the music changes (or stops) quickly find a partner. I'll call out either "folding," "faulting" or "layering." Show the process I name with the partner you've found. When the music changes again (or begins again), dance away from that partner. You will be working with a new partner each time you show a mountain-building process.

(Turn on music. If using a selection which has alternating sections, allow the music to continue to the end of the selection. If using a continuous selection, turn off the music each time you call out a mountain-building process.

When students are dancing freely it is very helpful to call out suggestions such as "Try moving backward or sideways...how about some high jumping or leaping...try some little movements and some big movements." Even experienced dancers need to be reminded of the many movement variations that are possible.

As pairs of students are showing folding, faulting or layering, call attention to some of the interesting variations that you see. For example: "Look how John and Robert are slowly pressing together as they fold." "Sarah and Jennifer had a really high volcanic eruption!")

Conclusion:

Today you had a chance to experience three different processes of mountain formation. Which one of these processes was the most fun for you to demonstrate? Why?

Variations:

If switching partners quickly is problematic for your class, you may have them return to the same partner each time. Be sure to encourage each pair to try new ways of demonstrating folding, faulting and layering every time they meet.

Extended Activities:

Ask individuals or small groups of students to research a specific mountain or mountain range to discover how it was formed. You may assign mountains, or ask students to choose their own.

Section C: Volcanoes

Throughout the course of the earth's history, volcanic activity has been changing the face of the earth. There have been hundreds of major eruptions and many thousands of minor eruptions since time began. These eruptions have taken lives, devastated landscapes, built mountains and created new land masses.

Volcanic activity occurs when molten material from the earth's interior bursts or flows to the surface of the earth. The material which escapes from a volcano may be in the form of lava, ash, gases, solid fragments of rock or any combination of these substances. Volcanic activity is caused by the buildup of heat and pressure deep within the earth.

Depending on the type of material which escapes from a volcano, different types of volcanic mountains are formed. Shield cones are gently rounded and are built almost entirely from lava flow. Cinder cones are small and steep and are created from volcanic cinders and ash. A composite cone is symmetrical with gentle lower slopes and steeper peaks. Composite cones are built when layers of lava are alternated with layers of cinders and ash.

In the lessons in this section students will discover, through movement, what causes volcanoes and will learn about the formation of three types of volcanic cones.

Lesson 30: What Causes Volcanic Activity?

Topic:
Causes of volcanic activity

Type of Movement Activity:
Large Group Improvisational Exploration

Related Movement Concepts:
Level (low, middle, high)
Weight (strong, light)
Flow (free, bound)

Materials / Preparation:
None

Musical Suggestions:
No music required

Space Requirements:
To do this activity as a large group, improvisational exploration requires a large, open space such as a gym, empty classroom, stage or outdoor area. Alternatively, a small group (five to eight students) could do the activity as a demonstration in an open area of the regular classroom.

Time Required:
Approximately 10 minutes

Introduction:

One of the most dramatic sights on the face of the earth is the eruption of a volcano. Hot lava may shoot high into the air and flow across the land for miles.

What causes a volcano to erupt? Deep within the earth's mantle is a molten substance called magma. Magma contains both hot, melted rock and gases. The gases in magma exert pressure on surrounding rock. As the magma rises it melts a pathway through the rock above it. When the rising magma reaches the earth's crust it accumulates in an underground pool called the ***magma chamber****.*

Inside the magma chamber, pressure begins to build. Finally the magma breaks through the earth's crust at weak spots, creating a large hole called the volcano's ***vent. Lava****, which is the name for magma which has reached the surface of the earth, spews through the vent. The vent may also spew out ashes, rocks and steam. The lava flows along the surface of the earth, then hardens.*

Lesson:

(Divide students into two groups, designating one group to represent magma and one to represent the rocks and crust of the earth.)

Would those of you who are in the "magma" group please come to the center of the space and get close together on a low level. You are hot magma deep under the surface of the earth.

Now I need the "rock and crust" group to come and surround the magma. Cover them with your arms, but make sure they have about two feet of space so they can rise before the volcano erupts.

Now the pressure within the magma is beginning to build. Magma, slowly begin to push your way up toward the crust of the earth. We should see you really using all of your muscles to press against the solid rock.

(The magma group rises until they are just underneath the arms of the students above them.)

Now the magma is forming a magma chamber underneath the crust. Magma, how can you show through movement that you are a hot, molten material? Would you move in a smooth flowing way like liquid? Would the heat cause you to shake or flick sharply?

The pressure inside the magma chamber is building. Magma, speed up your movements a little bit. Try twisting, swinging or vibrating quickly. When I say "erupt" you will push your way through the crust, jumping high into the air, then begin to flow as lava along the ground. Crust, when they erupt move quickly to the sides of the space so you won't be hurt.

(Magma group will push through the crust, jumping into the air then rolling and flowing along the ground. The crust group will have moved out of the way.)

Now the lava is flowing along the earth. Maybe it will flow in a curved pathway. As it cools it begins to slow down. Now let your lava harden into a shape. Will your hard lava shape be smooth and rounded or sharp and angular?

(Repeat the activity with reversed roles.)

Conclusion:

Today you experienced, through movement, how a volcano works. Who can describe in words the sequence of events that leads to a volcanic eruption?

Variations:

After describing the mechanics of a volcanic eruption to the entire class, break the class into small groups and allow them to find their own way to describe a volcanic eruption through movement.

You may want to combine this lesson with Lesson 31 on Volcanic Landforms.

Extended Activities:

Ask small groups of students to record a "live newscast" at the site of an imaginary volcanic eruption. They could describe the event before, during and after the eruption and interview witnesses. They might want to add music or sound effects to their recording.

Lesson 31: Volcanic Landforms

Topic:
Shield cone, Cinder cone, Composite cone

Type of Movement Activity:
Large Group Choreography

Related Movement Concepts:
Shape (straight, curved, angular, twisted)
Level (high, middle, low)
Flow (free, bound)

Materials / Preparation:
CD or tape player

Illustrations or photographs of a shield cone, a cinder cone and a composite cone (see next page)

Musical Suggestions:
Any selection from Discography

Space Requirements:
This activity requires adequate space for three large groups of students to work simultaneously. All three groups could work together in a single large, open space or each group could be assigned a separate space to work in, with the performance of the dances taking place at the front of the regular classroom.

Time Required:
Approximately 20 minutes

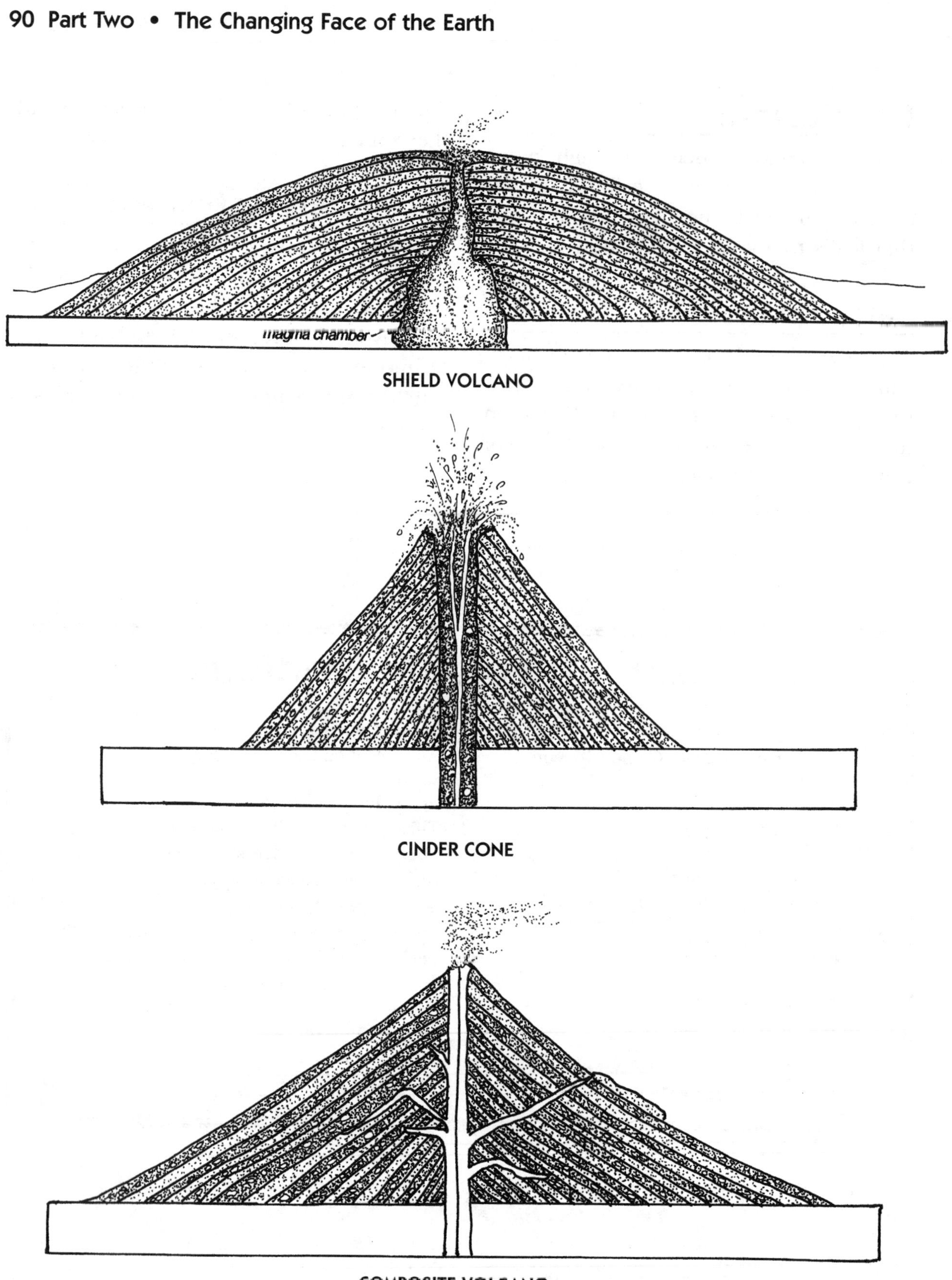

fig. 10 Volcanic Landforms

Introduction:

Although most volcanoes behave similarly, not every volcano looks the same. The shape of a volcano varies depending on the type of material that comes to the surface when the volcano erupts. The three basic volcanic landforms are ***shield cones, cinder cones*** *and* ***composite cones.***

Lesson:

The first type of volcano we'll learn about today is called a shield cone. *(Show photograph or illustration of a shield cone—see opposite page.)* Notice that the slopes of a shield cone are gentle and rounded rather than tall and steep. Shield cones are created entirely from lava which flows from the volcano and hardens in layers.

The group that choreographs about a shield cone will need to show us how the lava flows from the volcano's vent and hardens into a gently rounded mountain shape. We should see that the lava moves as a liquid, then hardens into a solid.

Now let's look at another type of volcano called a cinder cone. Cinder cones are smaller than shield cones and have steep sides. *(Show photograph or illustration of a cinder cone—see opposite page.)* Cinder cones are built entirely of settled cinders and ash.

The group that choreographs about a cinder cone will need to show us how cinder and ash erupt from the volcano's vent, then settle into a small, steep cone shape. Cinder and ash are very light, so perhaps they would float slowly before they settle.

The last volcanic landform we'll learn about is the composite cone. Composite cones are symmetrical, which means they look the same on all sides.

(Show photograph or illustration of a composite cone—see opposite page.)

The lower slopes of a composite cone are gentle, and are created by lava flow. The steeper center of a composite cone is formed of settling cinders and ash.

The group that choreographs about a composite cone will need to show us how the lava flows and hardens to create the base of the cone, and how cinders and ash settle to create the peak of the cone. In this movement study, we should see both the flowing liquid of the lava and the light floating of the cinders and ash.

(Divide the class into three groups, assigning each group one of the three volcanic landforms. Allow the groups approximately ten minutes to create movement studies describing the shape and formation of their landforms. Circulate among the groups providing assistance as needed.)

Conclusion:

Allow each group to perform in turn. At the end of each performance, ask the audience the following questions:

Which type of volcanic landform do you think this group was describing? Why do you think so?

How did the group show the type of material that formed their cone?

What Movement Concepts did this group use in creating their study?

Variations:

This activity could be done in smaller groups with two groups being assigned the same volcanic landform. It would be interesting to observe the differences in the way the two groups describe the same landform.

This lesson could be combined with Lesson 30: Causes of Volcanic Activity.

Extended Activities:

Have students create a three-dimensional model of a shield cone, cinder cone or composite cone using clay, plaster of Paris or paper mache. They could then paint the models to help show the type of material that formed the cone.

CONCLUDING LESSONS

These two lessons provide students with a review of some of the Earth Science concepts they have studied. Lesson 32 integrates science with creative writing, and may result in performance-quality movement pieces. Lesson 33 provides a concept and vocabulary review in the form of a guessing game.

Lesson 32: Natural Disasters

This lesson is based on a choreography idea by Anne Green Gilbert.

Topic:
Natural Disasters

Type of Movement Activity:
Small Group Choreography

Related Movement Concepts:
All Movement Concepts

Materials / Preparation:
Five pieces of paper, each with one of the following poems written on it. (see below)

Five pens or pencils

One extra copy of poem #1 (Volcano) written on chalkboard or butcher paper

Felt pen or chalk

Tape or CD player (optional)

Musical Suggestions:
Any selection from Discography (optional)

Space Requirements:
This activity requires adequate space for five groups of students to work simultaneously. The entire lesson could take place in a large, open space or it could be introduced in an open space with groups of students assigned to choreograph their dances in separate areas of the classroom or in various locations throughout the school building. The final performance of the dances could then take place in an open area of the regular classroom.

Time Required:
Approximately 30 minutes

Natural Disaster Poems

Volcano
Hot, Angry
______, ______, ______
Lava hardens into shapes
Volcano.

Earthquake
Sudden, Powerful
______, ______, ______
The ground shakes beneath our feet
Earthquake.

Tornado
Fast, Strong
______, ______, ______
Houses go swirling in the wind
Tornado.

Blizzard
Cold, White
______, ______, ______
Snowflakes flying everywhere
Blizzard.

Tsunami
Huge, Powerful
______, ______, ______
Water washes away cities
Tsunami.

Introduction:

Some events which take place on the earth are called "natural disasters." They are given this name because of the amount of destruction and hardship they can cause. Some events which are considered natural disasters are volcanoes, earthquakes, tornadoes, ***blizzards*** *and* ***tsunami****, which are huge ocean waves caused by earthquakes.*

Lesson:

Please take a look at the poem on the board describing a volcano. This type of poem is called a cinquain because it has five lines. Let's read the poem together:

Volcano
Hot, Angry
____, ____, ____
Lava hardens into shapes
Volcano.

As you can see, there are three words missing from the poem. I'm going to ask you to help me think of three verbs ending in i-n-g to put into the blanks. Examples might be: "steaming" or "erupting."

(Take suggestions from the students, then use the felt pen or chalk to write three appropriate i-n-g words in the blanks.)

Now let's work together to choreograph movement to this poem. What shall we do on the first line, which says "Volcano"?

(Take suggestions from the students. Possible solutions might be to have the entire class begin in the shape of a volcano, or for everyone to run to the center of the stage and make their own individual volcano shapes. Continue this decision-making process for every word or phrase of the poem, being sure to utilize student suggestions. A possible interpretation of the poem might be as follows:

VOLCANO: All make a group shape
HOT: All shake
ANGRY: All stomp
PRESSING: All press arms into air
STEAMING: All float from low to high level
ERUPTING: All leap into the air
LAVA HARDENS INTO SHAPES: All roll along the floor, then freeze in individual shapes
VOLCANO: All recreate original volcano shape

Allow students to perform the poem once as you read the words. This can be done with or without music.)

In a moment I'll divide the class into five groups and give each group a poem about a natural disaster. One group will get the volcano poem again, but they can choose new words and choreograph it very differently than we just did. The first thing you will need to do with your group is to read the poem and agree on three "i-n-g" words to write in the blanks. After you have completed the poem you will need to create movement to go along with it, just like we did for the volcano poem.

(Divide the class into five groups, giving each group a poem and a pen or pencil. Give the groups approximately fifteen minutes to fill in the blanks of the poem and decide how to interpret the poem in movement.)

Conclusion:

(Allow each group to perform their poem for the class, with or without music. You may read the poem as they perform or the group may choose to recite their poem as part of their performance.)

At the end of each performance ask the audience the following questions:

How successful was this group in portraying their particular natural disaster? Be specific in supporting your answer.

Which part of the poem did you find most exciting to watch? Why?

Which of the Movement Concepts did this group use in portraying their natural disaster?

Variations:

In working with a group that is inexperienced at writing, you may decide to have three verbs already written into the poems, or to leave only one blank for the group to fill in. For a more experienced group, you could give examples of the cinquain form, then allow them to write their own natural disaster poems.

Extended Activities:

You may want to use the students' natural disaster choreography as part of a performance for another class, or as part of a school assembly. You might also want to include it as part of a "Parent Education" evening about your innovative Earth Science program!

Lesson 33: Earth Science Review

Topic:
Earth Science Review

Type of Movement Activity:
Small Group Choreography

Related Movement Concepts:
All Movement Concepts

Materials / Preparation:
Ten 3x5 cards, each with one of the following written on it:

- Solid, liquid, gas
- Sedimentary rock
- Cumulonimbus cloud
- Cold and warm air masses meet
- Tornado
- High and low tide
- The water cycle
- Erosion
- Two earth plates converge and subduct
- Volcanic eruption

Each of these ten topics should also be written on the chalkboard or a large piece of butcher paper.

It is helpful for the students to have Earth Science textbooks, if applicable, or other Earth Science reference books available during this lesson.

Musical Suggestions:
No music required

Space Requirements:
This lesson would ideally take place in a large, open space such as an empty classroom, gym, stage or outdoor area. It is possible, however, to do this activity in the regular classroom by asking students to work on their movement studies in separate areas of the room or in other areas of the school building, then perform them in an open area of the regular classroom.

Time Required:
Approximately 25 minutes

Introduction:

In our study of Earth Science, we've covered many different topics from matter to the water cycle, from erosion to volcanoes.

Lesson:

We're going to play a guessing game today. In a minute I'll divide the class into groups of three or four. Each group will be assigned one of the Earth Science topics you see on the board. The group's job will be to show that topic so clearly in movement that the class will be able to guess which topic they were assigned.

Here are some questions your group might want to answer to help you in creating a short movement study about one of these topics: What is the most important information to remember about this topic, and how can we show that information in movement? Does the thing we are describing change or stay the same? What would be a logical way to begin and end the study? Which Movement Concepts would best help us describe this topic?

If you find that your group is having difficulty remembering information about your topic you are welcome to use your textbook *(if applicable)* or any Earth Science books in our classroom to research it. I will also be available to give help and answer any questions. I will give you approximately fifteen minutes to research your topic, discuss the topic with your group and create a short movement study on that topic.

> *(Divide the class into groups of three or four students, giving each group a card with one of the ten Earth Science topics written on it. Allow students approximately fifteen minutes to research, discuss and create their movement studies. Circulate among the groups, giving assistance as needed.)*

Conclusion:

Allow each group to perform in turn. Most of the studies will be quite short. At the end of each study, ask the audience the following questions:

> Which of the ten topics do you think this group was describing? Why do you think so?
>
> What important facts about this topic did the group include in their study?
>
> Which Movement Concepts did the group use to describe their topic?

Variations:

This activity could be done improvisationally with the class working in two teams. In this version of the activity the teacher would ask three students from Team A to come to the front of the room. These three students would be given a topic which they would describe in movement without pre-planning. Team A would receive points according to how quickly their teammates were able to guess which topic they were describing. The process would then be repeated with three members from Team B, and continued until all the topics had been described.

Extended Activities:

Ask the small groups to expand upon their topic by creating a piece of visual art, a poem, a short story, a tape recording or any other item that could be included in a classroom Earth Science display. Invite other classes, parents and administrators to share in the excitement that is generated when the arts are integrated into the curriculum!

Creating Your Own Movement-Based Science Lessons

(NOTE: The information in this chapter is based on a formula created by the author in collaboration with dance educator Eric Johnson.)

At this point it is my hope that you have successfully used many of the lessons in this book, and have experienced what a powerful teaching tool movement can be. You may even have had glimpses of other Earth Science topics, or even other areas of science study, for which movement would be a valuable method for reaching your students. If so, read on! In this chapter you will be given a formula for creating your own movement activities, which you can personally tailor to fit your curricular needs.

The first step in creating a movement-based science lesson is to choose a science topic that you wish to introduce, expand upon or review. Though a movement activity can be created to teach virtually any topic, some subjects lend themselves more easily to movement interpretation than others. In general, look for opportunities to describe a natural process such as erosion, volcanic eruption or the tides rather than simply state facts. As you read and research the topic, notice if any movement possibilities come to mind.

After you have chosen a science topic, decide what aspects of that topic you wish to focus on. In order to create a clear movement activity it is often necessary to simplify a subject area and bring it down to its essence. Don't worry about getting caught up in technical details, but look at the "big picture" of what natural process the topic relates to. Particularly look for elements that change, because change is what movement is all about.

Once you have chosen your topic and decided what aspects of it you wish to present, take a look at the listing of Movement Concepts which precedes the chapter "What Are Movement Concepts?" Peruse the list with your topic in mind and notice which concepts seem related. Is your lesson going to be about the Shape of an object, and perhaps how that shape changes? Does your lesson deal primarily with the way something moves through or occupies Space? Perhaps your lesson concerns the Quality of an object or process such as its Weight, Speed or Energy. Knowing which Movement Concepts are at play in your chosen scientific area of study will help you plan a meaningful activity.

Now you are familiar with your topic and with the Movement Concepts that relate to it. Your next step in creating your lesson is to decide what type of movement activity you wish to use. Begin by thinking about whether you wish to approach the topic through improvisation (creating movement "on the spot") or choreography (movement studies pre-planned by the students, which can later be performed.) In general, choreography requires more time than improvisation, especially if you wish students to share their finished work. Choreography also works most successfully with students who have had at least some previous experiences with improvisation. When you simply want to teach students about a scientific phenomenon, improvisation may be the best tool. When your goal is to have students synthesize their knowledge, draw comparisons or add their own interpretation to existing facts, choreography will most likely be the method you will want to use. (For more information on improvisation and choreography see the chapter "How to Use This Book").

The final decision you will need to make before actually planning your activity is whether the students will be working as individuals, with partners or in small or large groups. This decision should be made by looking both at what is most appropriate to your topic and to your students. Examine the topic and ask yourself if it concerns individual elements, relationships between two elements or between groups of elements. Evaluate your students and determine whether they are ready for a large group movement activity or would work most successfully as individuals. (For more information about student groupings, see the chapter "How to Use This Book.")

You now have a topic, have determined which Movement Concepts most closely relate to it, and have a sense of the type of movement activity and student grouping you plan to use. Now it's time to plan your lesson! Be sure that your lesson includes clear directions on what students are to do at all times, including transitions between sections of the lesson. You will want to introduce your subject simply before beginning the movement activity, and provide a concluding statement or review to signal the end of the lesson. As you plan, be sure to provide adequate time in your lesson for students to explore the scientific ideas in movement, and adequate flexibility to redirect students, simplify or expand on the activity if need be. To summarize, here are the steps you will follow in planning a movement-based science lesson:

Choose a science topic.
Decide which aspect(s) of the topic you will present.
Discern which Movement Concepts are related to the topic.
Choose the type of movement activity you will use:
- improvisational exploration
- choreography

Choose the student grouping you will use:
- individual
- partners
- small group (3–6 students)
- large group (more than 6 students)

Plan your activity, including an introduction, a conclusion and transitions.

To give an example of how I used the preceding formula to create one of the lessons in this book (Lesson 28: Earth Plate Movement), I began by choosing the topic "earth plates." In researching the topic, I decided that the changing relationships between two earth plates was the aspect that had the richest possibilities for movement. I noted that when earth plates move they have varying Relation-ships, in subducting they change Level and in colliding and sticking they move with different types of Energy. Therefore, I knew that my lesson needed to provide opportunities for the students to move using those concepts.

I decided to include both improvisational exploration and choreography in the lesson. I realized that I could quickly teach the three things that can occur when earth plates move through a simple partner improvisation. I then chose to allow the students to use their own aesthetic sense to pre-plan (choreograph) a sequence in which to do those three movements.

Though I could have chosen to make this a group rather than a partner activity, I decided that working in partners would be the simplest and most effective way to present the material. In other words, several students could have joined together to form one earth plate but it would have complicated the activity and would not have helped to elucidate the topic. (Note also that I chose to have the two students meet while standing rather than while lying down. Though having the students lie on the floor would have been more "technically correct," it could also have been a source of space and management problems, as well as making the movement more difficult.)

Creating a Movement-Based Science Lesson with Students

After becoming comfortable with the process of creating movement-based science lessons on your own, you may want to try creating a movement / science activity in collaboration with your students. To accomplish this, use the preceding formula but ask students to contribute their ideas at each step. You could do this together as a class discussion, or give students the formula and ask them to create an activity on their own or with a small group. You will doubtless be surprised at the originality of their ideas, and the enthusiasm that will be generated in allowing them to take part in the design of their own learning activities.

For many teachers planning a movement activity is a new experience, and can be somewhat threatening. Start simply, pay attention to what works, change —without self-judgment—what doesn't work. The earth is always changing, as is science, as is education, as are you as an educator. When you open your classroom to the possibility of learning through movement, you are giving your students the gift of becoming active participants in their own quest for knowledge.

Glossary

abrasion—the scraping of one substance against another.

air mass—a large body of air which is about the same temperature and humidity all the way through.

anticline—the upward-arching part of a folded rock.

atmosphere—the gases and particles that surround the earth's lithosphere and hydrosphere, composed mainly of nitrogen and oxygen.

atom—the smallest component of an element which contains all the properties of that element.

blizzard—a storm characterized by large amounts of snow.

choreography—a pre-planned movement sequence, or the act of planning such a sequence.

chemical weathering—a change in the actual composition of a material due to exposure to a foreign substance.

cinder cone—a small, steep volcanic mountain formed from settled cinders and ash.

cirrus—a thin, wispy cloud formed of ice crystals.

cleavage—the ability of a mineral to break into smooth, parallel surfaces.

climate—the average weather conditions in a particular region.

composite cone—a volcanic mountain formed from a combination of lava, cinders and ash.

compound—a substance that is made up of two or more elements joined together.

condensation—the changing of a gas into a liquid.

continental margin—the region of the ocean bottom that separates a continent from the sea floor.

continental rise—base of a continental margin.

continental shelf—flat shelf of land at the top of a continental margin.

continental slope—the part of the continental margin that slopes steeply toward the ocean floor.

convergence—the meeting of two earth plates, usually causing the formation of mountain ranges and deep trenches.

crawl—to move along the floor on one's belly.

creep—to walk on one's hands and knees.

cross-lateral—two-sided movement, as in stepping forward with the right leg while reaching forward with the left arm.

crust—the rigid, solid outer layer of the earth; part of the lithosphere.

cumulonimbus—tall, dark cumulus clouds that produce thunderstorms.

cumulus—a puffy cloud formed when warm, moist air is forced upward.

delta—a fan-shaped area of land located at the mouth of a river, formed when the river deposits sediment.

deposition—the laying down of particles of earth materials by an agent of erosion.

divergence—the spreading apart of earth plates, leaving a gap which then fills with molten material from under the earth's surface.

element—a substance made up of only one type of atom.

erosion—the carrying away of rock and soil by running water, glaciers, wind or gravity.

evaporation—the changing of a liquid into a gas.

experimentation—the controlled testing of hypotheses.

fault—a crack or fracture in rock.

faulting—the movement of rocks along a crack.

floodplain—the wide, flat area covered by a mature river which has worn away most of its banks.

folding—the bending of rock due to high pressure.

fracture—the tendency of a mineral to break into surfaces that are not flat, such as a crystal which breaks into smooth, rounded surfaces.

front—the area where two different air masses meet.

gas—matter that is in a state in which molecules are far apart and move freely, as in steam.

geologist—an earth scientist who specializes in the study of rocks and minerals.

glacier—a large, moving mass of ice and snow.

groundwater—water that has filtered through the earth's surface.

guyot—a low, flat-topped underwater mountain.

hardness—the ability of a mineral to withstand scratching by another mineral or object such as a nail.

homolateral—movement of one side of the body at a time, as in moving the right arm and right leg simultaneously.

humidity—the amount of moisture in the air.

hydrosphere—all of the earth's water, including atmospheric moisture and underground water.

hypothesis—a possible answer to a question, formed through observation.

igneous rock—rock which is formed from magma.

impermeable rock—rock that will not allow water to pass through.

improvisation—the spontaneous performance of movement without preplanning.

inference—an interpretation or explanation of an observed pattern.

inner core—the innermost layer of the earth which is extremely hot and under great pressure.

interior—the part of the earth which is beneath the crust, composed of molten material.

ion—electrified atom.

ionosphere—upper layer of the earth's atmosphere, containing electrified atoms known as ions.

kinesthetic—referring to physical sensations experienced by the body through touch and movement.

Laban Movement Analysis—a system of describing, notating and analyzing movement, as developed by Rudolph von Laban. Born in the late 1880s, Laban did most of his work in movement analysis in the 1930s and 1940s and died in 1958.

lava—magma which reaches the surface of the earth as a result of a volcanic eruption.

liquid—matter that is in a state in which molecules have some space between them, allowing the substance to flow, as in water.

lithosphere—the rigid crust and upper mantle of the earth, composed of rock and soil.

locomotor—traveling movement; movement that transports the body from one place to another in space, such as walking, running and so on.

magma—molten liquid rock found beneath the earth's surface.

magma chamber—underground pool of lava beneath the earth's crust.

mantle—the layer of matter extending from the earth's core outward to the crust.

mass—the amount of material in something.

matter—that which occupies space and has mass.

meanders—curves caused by the wearing away of the banks on either side of a river.

metamorphic rock—rock which has been changed from one type to another by heat and pressure.

mineral—a naturally occurring substance found in the earth's crust and upper mantle which consists of a single compound or element.

mixture—a substance made up of two or more elements or compounds, which can be separated into parts.

molecule—microscopic particle of a substance, containing one or two atoms.

moraine—material, usually rocks and boulders, picked up by a glacier as it moves and deposited as it melts.

non-locomotor—stationary movement; movement that does not transport the body from one place to another in space such as bending, twisting, swinging and so on.

observation—using the senses to receive information; looking closely.

outer core—the layer of the earth between the inner core and mantle which contains liquid iron and nickel.

ozone layer—atmospheric layer, located at the upper edge of the stratosphere, which filters out the sun's ultraviolet rays and prevents them from reaching the earth.

pattern—a sequence of events or objects which occurs repeatedly.

physical weathering—the breaking down of earth materials into smaller fragments due to atmospheric forces, abrasion or pressure from the roots of plants and trees.

plate tectonic theory—the theory that the earth's surface is made up of rigid, slowly moving plates.

precipitation—water that falls from the atmosphere to the surface of the earth in the form of rain, snow or hail.

property—a feature of a substance, including color, size, weight, taste, shape, texture and smell.

rock cycle—the cycle of changes from one class of rock to another.

runoff—the flow of water off the earth's surface.

sand dune—crescent-shaped mound of sand deposited by wind in the desert.

seamount—underwater volcanic cone that may reach the ocean's surface to form an island.

sediment—small pieces of rock formed when larger rocks are broken up by rain, running water, earthquakes or wind.

sedimentary rock—rock which is formed from particles of other rocks and minerals or the remains of living organisms that have been deposited in one place and pressed into layers.

shield cone—a gently sloping volcanic mountain formed by lava flow.

solid—matter that is in a state in which molecules are very close together.

stratosphere—layer of the earth's atmosphere located above the troposphere; where airplanes fly.

stratus—a type of cloud which is flat and layered, formed where a layer of warm air and a layer of cool air meet.

streak—the color left behind when a mineral is rubbed against a flat piece of unglazed porcelain.

subduction—when one earth plate moves beneath another.

syncline—the section of folded rock which dips downward.

talus—pile of rocks deposited at the bottom of a mountain by gravity.

theory—a tested hypothesis which is generally accepted as fact.

tide—the rise and fall of the level of the ocean at a particular location during the course of a single day, caused by the gravitational pull of the moon on the earth.

transform—the movement of two earth plates past one another.

trench—long, deep underwater canyon, usually surrounded by volcanoes.

troposphere—layer of the earth's atmosphere containing most of the atmosphere's oxygen and all of its life, which extends six to ten miles above the earth.

tsunami—huge ocean wave caused by an earthquake or other earth movements.

ultraviolet—electromagnetic energy waves in sunlight that can cause suntanning and sunburn and are partially filtered out by the atmosphere.

vapor—water in a gaseous state.

vent—opening at the top of a volcano through which lava escapes.

vestibular system—one of three systems that helps us to know where we are in space (the others being vision and proprioception—knowing where one part of the body is in relation to the rest.) The vestibular system consists of a semicircular canal with several loops, located in each inner ear. These canals are lined with tiny hairs and are partially filled with a gelatinous fluid that is sloshed or disturbed every time the body moves. This fluid is drawn toward the earth by the pull of gravity so that, depending on where our heads are oriented at the time, those hairs nearest to the ground are stimulated more than those that are further away from it. This helps us sense our relationship to the earth.

water cycle—the cycling of water from the earth's surface to the atmosphere and back through the processes of evaporation and precipitation.

water table—the upper boundary of the water-saturated soil known as the "zone of saturation."

weather—the constantly changing temperature, wind activity and moisture content of the air at any given point in time.

weathering —the breaking down of the earth's rocks into smaller particles by the atmosphere.

Discography

Each lesson in this book suggests using a musical selection from one of the four categories listed below. You may use one of the specific selections listed or substitute a favorite of your own. There is a separate listing of recordings that were created especially for use in teaching Creative Dance.

Constant, dense

Jarre, Jean Michel, *Oxygene* (any selection) Polydor, PD-1-6112.

Jones, Peter and Podlesny, Joe, "The Land of Nod," *The Fifth Movement*, Four Zoa Music.

Roth, Gabrielle and the Mirrors, "Red Wind," *Totem*, Raven Recording, LC5565.

Satie, Eric, "Gymnopedies," *Windham Hill Sampler '81,* WH1015.

Tjapukai Dancers, "Kakadu," *Proud to be Aborigine*, Jarra Hill Records, CDJHR2012.

Flowing

Dietrichson, Tor, "Global Village," *Global Village*, Global Pacific Records, WK 40728.

Enya, "Caribbean Blue," *Shepherd Moons,* Reprise Records, 4-26775.

Haun, Steve, "The Constant Search," *Inside the Sky*, Silver Wave Records, SR-504.

Jarre, Jean Michel, *The Essential Jarre* (any selection), PRO L.

Vollenweider, Andreas, "The Glass Hall," *White Winds*, CBS FMT 39963.

Energetic, driving

Day Parts, "Morning Blend," *Sunday Morning Coffee*, American Gramaphone Records, AGCD100.

Dead Can Dance, "Bird," *A Passage in Time*, Ryko, RCD 20215.

Gynt, Peer, "In the Hall of the Mountain King," *Incidental Music for Ibsen's Drama*, Angel 4XS-36531.

Penguin Café Orchestra, "Music for a Found Harmonium," *Broadcasting From Home*, Editions EG, EGEDC 38.

Shadowfax, "Another Country," *Dreams of Children*, WH-1038.

Light, airy

Day Parts, "Across the View," *Sunday Morning Coffee*, American Gramaphone Records, AGCD100.

Deuter, "Call of the Unknown," *Call of the Unknown*, Celestial Harmonies, LC 2099.

Lynch, Ray, "Celestial Soda Pop," *Deep Breakfast*, RLLP-102.

Nakai, R. Carlos, *Earth Spirit* (any selection), Canyon Records, CR-612 Volume 4.

Roth, Gabrielle and the Mirrors, "Dolphin," *Bones*, Raven Recording.

Shadowfax, "Dreams of Children," *Dreams of Children*, WH 1038.

Music for Creative Dance

Chappelle, Eric, *Music for Creative Dance: Contrast and Continuum, Volumes I and II* (all selections), Ravenna Ventures, Inc., RVCD 9301 and 9401. (NOTE: These two CDs contain many selections with alternating phrases, and are excellent for use in exploring the Movement Concepts.)

Barlin, Anne, "Freeze and Move," *Hello Toes: Movement Games for Children*, Princeton Book Company.

For information on ordering Eric Chappelle's *Music for Creative Dance: Contrast and Continuum, Volumes I and II* write or call:

Ravenna Ventures, Inc.
4756 University Village Pl. NE. #117
Seattle, WA. 98105
(206) 528-7556

Bibliography

Books About Earth Science

Dickey, John S., Jr. 1988. *On the Rocks*. New York: John Wiley and Sons, Inc.

Fariel, Robert E. and Hinds, Robert W. 1984. *Earth Science*. Addison Wesley Publishing Company, Inc.

Levenson, Elaine. 1994. *Teaching Children About Life and Earth Sciences*. New York: TAB Books.

Marshall, Robert H. and Rosskopf, Allen. 1994. *Earth Science*. Circle Pines, Minn.: American Guidance Service, Inc.

Maynard, Christopher. 1974. *Planet Earth*. Great Britain: Sampson Low.

Parker, Steve. 1989. *The Earth and How It Works*. London: Dorling Kindersley, Inc.

Rowe, Mary Budd. 1973. *Teaching Science as Continuous Inquiry*. New York: McGraw Hill Book Company.

Books on Movement and the Brain

Ayres, Jean A., Ph.D. 1972. *Sensory Integration and Learning Disorders*. Western Psychological Services.

Delacato, Carl H. 1977. *A New Start for the Child with Reading Problems*. New York: Macmillian.

Gardner, Howard. 1983, *Frames of Mind: the Theory of Multiple Intelligences*. New York: New York University Press.

Lewinn, Dr. Edward D. 1977. *Human Neurological Organization.* Springfield, Ill.: Charles C. Thomas Publishers.

For further information on Movement and the Brain, write to:

Bette Lamont, Director
Developmental Movement Center
10303 Meridian Ave. N. Suite 201
P.O. Box 75681
Seattle, Wash. 98125

Books on the Work of Rudolph von Laban

Bartenieff, Irmgaard, with Lewis, Dori. 1980. *Body Movement: Coping With the Environment*. New York: Gordon and Breach Science Publishers.

Laban, Rudolph von. 1963. *Modern Educational Dance*, Second Edition. London: MacDonald and Evans.

For further information on the work of Rudolph von Laban, write to:

Laban-Bartenieff Institute for Movement Studies
11 East 4th Street 3rd Floor
New York, NY 10003

BOOKS ON TEACHING CREATIVE MOVEMENT AND DANCE

Gilbert, Anne Green. 1992. *Creative Dance for All Ages*. Reston, Virginia: American Alliance for Health, Physical Education, Recreation and Dance.

Gilbert, Anne Green. 1977. *Teaching the Three R's Through Movement Experiences*. Minneapolis, Minn: Burgess Publishing Company.

Joyce, Mary. 1994. *First Steps in Teaching Creative Dance to Children*, Third Edition. Mountain View, Calif.: Mayfield Publishing Company.

Landalf, Helen and Gerke, Pamela. 1996. *Movement Stories for Young Children Ages 3-6*. Lyme, New Hampshire: Smith and Kraus, Inc.

Sample Creative Dance Lesson One

Movement Concept: Speed (slow, medium, fast)
Length of Lesson: 45 minutes

Warm-up:

Have students mirror (copy) your self-space (stationary) movements. Begin with slow movements such as stretching, slow twisting and swaying. Gradually accelerate the movements. If you are uncomfortable leading this warm-up, ask a student to be the leader.

Musical Suggestion: Chappelle, Eric, "Adagio for Two Violins," *Music for Creative Dance: Contrast and Continuum, Volume I.*

Concept Introduction:

Introduce students to the concept Speed by having them move their arms very slowly, at a medium speed, then very quickly as they say the words "slow, medium, fast."

Concept Exploration:

Play a musical selection with alternating sections of slow and fast tempos. When the music is slow ask students to move through space as slowly as they can in different directions, on different levels, etc. When the music is fast, ask the students to find many ways to move quickly. During the next section of slow music, challenge the students to move their legs slowly (walking, floating, etc.) and their arms and upper bodies quickly (i.e.: shaking, poking, etc.). On the next musical change, ask them to do the opposite: move the upper body slowly and the lower body quickly.

Musical Suggestion: Chappelle, Eric, "Western East." *Music for Creative Dance: Contrast and Continuum, Volume I.*

Skill Development:

Create a movement sentence that accelerates, i.e.: stretch, melt, roll, rise, skip, shake, explode. Teach the sequence to your students and have them try it several times. Then try reversing the sequence.

Musical Suggestion: Lynch, Ray, "Celestial Soda Pop," *Deep Breakfast.*

Place small traffic cones or milk cartons on the floor in a line or horseshoe formation. Ask students to leap over them, alternating slow, floating leaps with quick, bursting leaps.

Musical Suggestion: Chappelle, Eric, "Jammin' On the Porch," *Music for Creative Dance: Contrast and Continuum, Volume I.*

Improvisation:

Play short selections of music from different countries. Ask students to move spontaneously to each selection and freeze in a shape between selections. Encourage them to move in contrast to the tempo of the music as well as to duplicate the tempos they hear.

Musical Suggestion: Barlin, Anne, "Freeze and Move," *Hello Toes.*

Sample Creative Dance Lesson Two

Movement Concept: Balance (on, off)
Length of Lesson: 1 hour

Warm-up:

Turn on some lively music and allow students to move freely. Guide them by suggesting different movements they might try: skipping, stretching, turning, slashing, etc. When the music pauses, students must find a balancing shape (i.e.: balancing on one foot) and hold it until the music begins again.

Musical Suggestions: Chappelle, Eric, "Chirpa, Chirpa," *Music for Creative Dance: Contrast and Continuum, Volume I.*

Concept Introduction:

Introduce students to the concept Balance by having them try several shapes which are On Balance—very stable and grounded—then tipping those shapes so they are Off Balance.

Concept Exploration:

With students spread out in the room, call out a math equation such as "twelve divided by four." Each student must respond by creating a shape balancing on three body parts, i.e.: two hands and one foot. You may ask them to try moving this shape through space. Continue with other equations. *(Note: Thank you to Anne Green Gilbert for this activity.)*

Musical Suggestion: Chappelle, Eric, "Oasis," *Music for Creative Dance: Contrast and Continuum: Volume I.*

Developing Skills:

Have students practice the following movement combination, beginning with each students standing across the room from a partner:

Skip and trade places with your partner.
Slide to meet your partner in the middle of the room.
Create three balancing shapes with your partner.
Leap apart, returning to your original starting place.

(Note: This sequence may be performed to specific counts, or on the student's own timing.)

Musical Suggestions: Chappelle, Eric, "Bee Beat," *Music for Creative Dance: Contrast and Continuum, Volume II.*

Have students leap over cones or milk cartons, then create a spectacular balancing shape at the end of the leaping course.

Choreography:

Ask trios (three students) or quartets (four students) to create dances in an A-B-A form: A = balance together, B = dance apart, A = balance together. After planning and practicing their dances, allow each group to perform their dance for the class. Ask audience members to give the dancers specific, positive feedback about their balancing shapes, and to name the Movement Concepts they observed as the dancers moved apart.

Musical Suggestions: Chappelle, Eric, "Whales," *Music for Creative Dance: Contrast and Continuum, Volume II.*